2006

HAROLD & WILLIAM

HAROLD&WILLIAM

THE BATTLE FOR ENGLAND 1064-1066

BENTON RAIN PATTERSON

TEMPUS

First published 2001
This edition first published 2004

Tempus Publishing Limited
The Mill, Brimscombe Port,
Stroud, Gloucestershire, GL5 2QG
www.tempus-publishing.com

British Library Cataloguing in Publication Data.
A catalogue record for this book is available from the British Library.

ISBN 0 7524 2984 1

Typesetting and origination by Tempus Publishing Limited
Printed in Great Britain by Midway Colour Print, Wiltshire

CONTENTS

	Introduction	7
1	The Royal Mission, Summer 1064	15
2	The Proposition, Summer 1064	23
3	The Unintended Oath, Summer 1064	29
4	The King, Summer 1064	33
5	The Rebellion, Summer 1064–Autumn 1065	37
6	The Crowned Head, November 1065–January 1066	47
7	The Overseas Reaction, January 1066	57
8	The Channel, Prehistory to 1066	61
9	The War Plan, January 1066–February 1066	69
10	The Preparations, February 1066–April 1066	77
11	The Papal Decision, Spring 1066	89
12	The Betrayal, Spring 1066	95
13	The Hard Man, June 1066	103

14   The Long Wait, July 1066   109

15   The Land Ravager, July 1066–September 1066   113

16   The Stamford Bridge, September 1066   125

17   The Norman Fleet, September 1066   139

18   The Pevensey Landing, September 1066   145

19   The Omen, October 1066   151

20   The Opposing Hills, 12 October–14 October 1066   157

21   The Battle, 14 October 1066   167

22   The Aftermath, 15 October–25 December 1066   177

      Chronology   180

      About the Book's Sources   183

      Selected Bibliography   187

      Index   189

INTRODUCTION

Historians have generally treated the year 1066 as a year of beginnings. And of course it was, marking as it did the beginning of new political and social regimes in England and new international relationships, the beginning of the imposition of Norman influences on English warfare, law and architecture, the beginning of a monarchy that has reigned now going on 1,000 years, and not the least significant of all, the beginning of the superimposition of the Normans' French language upon English. It's proper that the year of the Norman Conquest has been offered in such a light, since those beginnings have more relevance to today than does all that they replaced.

But of course the beginnings are not the whole story of the conquest, which was equally an end, and a tragic, sad one at that. The wrong side, the wrong cause, the wrong man won. The right side, the right cause, the right man lost.

Human nature has within it some romantic quality that finds attraction in vanished worlds and failed causes. Or why else do sights of Pompeii's ruins or of *Titanic*'s wreck move us so, and stories of Camelot and of Tara cause our hearts to yearn? The defeat of Harold Godwinson and his gallant army of Englishmen, fighting in defence of their homes, their country and their freedom, has for more than twenty years held the same sort of melancholic fascination for me. I keep thinking of what might have been if just one vital link in the chain of fateful events had been different. I mourn that day – Saturday 14 October 1066 – when on the bloodied slope of Senlac Ridge, near Hastings, England, events took a horribly wrong turn and a good and brave man, overwhelmed by a confluence of misfortunes, lost his most important battle, lost his kingdom and his life, all in one tragic moment.

As a writer, I felt that the tragedy of Hastings was too poignant to be ignored and Harold was too heroic to be remembered only as England's last Anglo-Saxon king. He deserved to have his story told, not merely the story of the Battle of Hastings or even of that whole disastrous year, but the story of the man himself and how it was that he came to his monumentally historic moment on Senlac Ridge.

I had – still have – an abundance of sympathy for Harold. I identified with him. The conflict between him and William, between Englishmen and Normans, was a clear case of us against them, and my British Isles ancestry, antedating the Norman Conquest, made me, like Harold, one of the us. Harold and his soldiers, most of them militiamen, citizen soldiers, were fighting in noble defence of their homes, their families and their country; William and his army were fighting to subjugate the people of England and confiscate their country. The conflict was a mammoth struggle between right and wrong. Harold embodied the right.

Ethnic attachments and moral issues aside, Harold was the more winsome personality, the more likeable person. He wasn't a bully or a braggard, which William was. He wasn't cruel or tyrannical, which William was. And if Harold was an opportunist, William was even more so. If Harold was overly ambitious, William was many times more so. If Harold violated an oath made to William, I believed he was justified in having done so. To my way of thinking, Harold was simply a more admirable person, a nicer guy than William, and I just liked him better. He was my sentimental favourite, and I pulled for him.

Propelled by such feelings, I determined to show Harold to an audience of readers and have them know and appreciate him. I wanted to write this story with the unhappy ending and make it as complete and readable as I was able.

It didn't take long to run into the problems of attempting such a feat. The biggest – and it loomed huge – was a paucity of material, particularly on Harold. There were one-volume biographies on William (David C. Douglas's *William the Conqueror*) and on the man who might be called the main supporting actor in the drama of Harold and William, King Edward the Confessor (Frank Barlow's *Edward the Confessor*), but the only book-size biographies of Harold contained more fiction than fact (Hope Muntz's novel, *The Golden Warrior*, and Lord Bulwer-Lytton's novel, *Harold, Last of the Saxon Kings*). Would-be Harold biographers evidently couldn't find enough information about him to make an entire book in the way that Douglas and Barlow had done with their subjects. The records, meagre as they were, lacked even such basic details as the year Harold was born (and thus his age) and what he looked like. Also lacking were details on some of the major events in his life, including how he happened to become the apparent captive of the count of Ponthieu, how he managed to rescue one or more of William's soldiers, what the extent of his involvement was in William's campaign in Brittany. Such missing details would make the story hard to tell without resort to vagueness and speculation. Direct quotes from Harold – things he said or wrote – were, with a couple of exceptions that sprang from legend, virtually non-existent. Dialogue couldn't be done, and thus it was next to impossible to get to know him from his own words. I could see why Muntz and Bulwer-Lytton had chosen fiction to paint their portraits of Harold.

A second large problem was the trustworthiness of the material that was available. Norman accounts, with their absurd exaggerations and allegations, were obviously suspect. Norman writers, whose major purpose was to justify William's bloody aggrandisement, zealously demonised Harold and beatified William. The conqueror's sycophantic chaplain, William of Poitiers, who in the early 1070s wrote an account of the conquest (*The Deeds of William, Duke of the Normans and King of the English*), a document that otherwise might be considered a primary source, told his English readers that 'if only you would cast aside your foolishness and wickedness, you would love... the man who now has power over you, for he removed from your neck the proud and cruel despotism of Harold and killed the hateful tyrant who had reduced you to ruinous and shameful slavery'. In another passage, he describes Harold as 'stained with vice, a cruel murderer, purse-proud and puffed up with the profits of pillage'.

Probably the most widely known and perhaps the most influential account of the Harold-William drama is the vivid and imaginative Bayeux Tapestry, the 231-foot-long, twenty-inch-wide embroidery creation that is today publicly displayed in Bayeux, the city in Normandy where in the eleventh century Duke William's half-brother Odo was bishop. The tapestry was commissioned by Odo and designed by Norman artists to serve as an elaborate piece of Norman propaganda. Its pictorial story of Harold and William and the events leading up to and including the Battle of Hastings is an historic treasure of authentic eleventh-century detail such as dress and armour and weaponry, but what it tells of Harold is open to serious question. The tapestry's depiction of Harold's voyage to Normandy in 1064, his subsequent capture by Count Guy of Ponthieu and his rescue by Duke William, all vital to accounting for Harold's supposed obligation to William, provides a singular example of its questionableness. Those episodes, which are also recounted by William of Poitiers and by another of Duke William's Norman biographers, William of Jumièges (*The Deeds of the Duke of the Normans*), are roundly disputed by Edwin Tetlow in his keenly analytical work, *The Enigma of Hastings*, published in 1974. Tetlow argues that the entire sequence of pictured events is a fabrication, a fraud committed by William's talented eleventh-century apologists. Tetlow offers evidence that Harold did indeed travel across the Channel but that the trip was made in 1056 rather than 1064, and that Harold was Count Guy's guest, not his prisoner. The tapestry, Tetlow says, 'might represent a most skilful adaptation and extension of the true facts'. Suspicions about those depicted events cast shadows of doubt over other parts of the tapestry's account, the most significant of which is the oath alleged to have been made by Harold to William. That oath, by which Harold promised to support William's claim to the English throne, was to become the key element in William's public relations campaign against Harold and his primary justification for his brutal conquest.

In addition to the malicious distortions and other falsifications by William's supporters, the written material on the two men includes details that sprang not from verifiable fact but from legend. Some of the material has the obvious look of legend, believable perhaps to readers and listeners of the eleventh century but giving cause for scepticism today. An example is the tale of the Waltham Abbey statue of Christ that lowered its head in response to Harold's prayer.

Some of the legendary material, though having originated years after the events involved and thus being suspect, has been made acceptable by verisimilitude and the passage of time. Some of it is colourful and hard to resist. There is, for instance, the account of the Battle of Stamford Bridge written by Snorri Sturluson more than 150 years after its occurrence. In his saga, *Heimskringla*, Snorri recreates dialogue between Harold and his brother Tostig as their armies are about to face-off in mortal combat. That material and other Harold quotes are absolutely precious. It seems highly probable that Snorri wrote, from an oral tradition, the legend of the exploits of King Harald Hardrada. His account has the colour of authenticity and has been accepted as authoritative, by this author and others, even though recorded a century and a half after the fact.

Once the research was done – or at least the bulk of it – I sat surveying a new set of considerations. There was the matter of perspective to be decided. Until I was very near starting to write, I had thought of this story as Harold's story, and so the action would be seen by the reader from Harold's perspective. But William was too integral a character in the last two years of Harold's life, and I finally decided Harold must share the spotlight with his adversary. The story would be told from both perspectives.

Another question was, where should the story begin? It wasn't meant to be a biography. It was to be the story of these two men's rivalry for the throne of England. The story then should start, I reasoned, at the beginning of the rivalry, with the circumstances that first drew Harold and William together.

I decided to begin at that point – which was, according to most accounts, in 1064 when Harold was dispatched by King Edward on a mission to William in Normandy. That decision of mine immediately presented the next problem: how to handle discrepancies. As appealing as I found Edwin Tetlow's argument for an earlier date for Harold's trip and as agreeable as I was to Tetlow's charges of falsification in the Norman accounts, I concluded that there must be some truth in the traditional story of Harold's having embarked on King Edward's mission, having suffered misfortune *en route* and having ended up in a compromised position on the other side of the English Channel.

Other discrepancies and historically disputed events I would decide either on the basis of what the majority of previous writers had concluded or on what seemed most reasonable. In some instances, such as the discrepancies in estimates of the size of the armies, I would decide by choosing the middle ground between the extremes of earlier writers. I wanted very much to avoid repeatedly telling the reader, in effect, 'Some experts say this, but on the other hand, others say that.' And so I picked a figure, one that was, I believed, reasonable and from an authoritative source.

I thought the best, most effective way to tell the story was as narrative. What I mean by 'narrative' is telling the story by describing the action, the scenes and the characters and letting readers see, feel, hear for themselves rather than having information filtered through and summarised by the writer in the form of exposition (as in this introduction). As every storyteller knows, narrative is more readable than exposition, and I wanted the story to be as readable as the facts and reasonable speculation would permit.

The next difficulty: gaps in the story. In parts of the story there was not much in the historical record to go on. Authentic scenes would be hard to reproduce without actual details. If I started where I intended – Harold's departure for William's capital at Rouen – the story would begin with what was a gap in the historical record. How much licence could I take to fill the gap? In the first volume of his massive, eleven-volume *The Story of Civilization*, Will Durant sets forth the proposition that 'most history is guessing' (*Our Oriental Heritage*, page 12). I like that proposition, as well as another that is also Durant's: '... all history should be taken as hypothesis... of yesterday there is no certainty' (*The Age of Reason Begins*, page 607). Durant seems to be saying that writing history requires at least some speculation, and so I began to feel justified in employing it in the story of Harold and William. But whatever guesswork was to be included would have to be founded on strong probability and known concomitant facts. Speculation, moreover, would be labelled as such.

The final matter to be resolved was where the story should end. Since it was not so much a story of the conquest as of the two men themselves, I decided it should end not with England's submission nor with William's coronation. It should end where the rivalry ended, on the battlefield. If that left readers feeling down, well, that's the way they were expected to feel. It was the way I felt.

For a long time I couldn't help wondering if the conflict had to turn out the way it did. Was Harold destined to fail and William to succeed?

Or could there have been a different outcome? Looking back, seeing all that transpired, on both sides of the Channel, one does get a feeling of preordination. Perhaps one pondering the events preceding and the outcome of the battle might even admit the possibility of the explanation offered by the author of *The Anglo-Saxon Chronicles*, who wrote that 'the French held the field of the dead as God granted them because of the people's sins'.

Yet one can see what a difference was made by the treason of Harold's brother Tostig, precipitating as it did King Harald Hardrada's invasion and the exhausting Battle of Stamford Bridge just days before Harold faced William on Senlac Ridge. Without having had to first overcome the Norse invaders, Harold's army doubtless would have been a more formidable, perhaps indomitable, force on Senlac Ridge, had its placement on the Channel coast even allowed William to progress that far.

And without William's incredible good fortune with the vagaries of autumn weather and the English Channel and his fleet's remarkable survival of the storm into which it sailed upon leaving the River Dives estuary, certainly the story would have had a different end.

But all those things were beyond Harold's control. There was nothing he could have done about them. On the other hand, there were things he could have done – and now we know he *should* have done – that in all likelihood would have given history a different outcome. There were alternatives to the immediate, one big battle, personal showdown that Harold was determined to have with William.

(History buffs may contrast Harold's action with the strategy of General George Washington in the eighteenth century. Washington's situation as commander-in-chief of America's continental army and militias, defending their homeland against a seaborne invasion by a well-equipped, disciplined foreign army, is an approximate parallel to Harold's. Washington summarised his strategy in a letter to the president of the Continental Congress dated 8 September 1776: '... on our side the war should be defensive... we should on all occasions avoid a general action or put anything to the risk, unless compelled by a necessity, into which we ought never to be drawn'.)

The alternatives available to Harold were pointed out to him by his brother Gyrth, who urged him to take one or more of them. Harold, his head losing the argument to his emotions, stubbornly refused.

Instead, against his brother's wise counsel and what should have been his own better judgement, he bet it all at Senlac Ridge, including his life.

It was an enormous mistake.

What happened, I now believe, didn't have to happen. And in that sad fact lies the real tragedy of the story of Harold and William.

B.R.P.

I

THE ROYAL MISSION
SUMMER 1064

I n the summer of the year 1064, on a day unnoticed by the chroni-
clers of great events, Harold Godwinson, the second most important man in all of England, boarded a ship and embarked on a
mission that would ultimately change his nation forever and would
influence world history for many centuries.

Still robust at about the age of forty-three, father of three teenage
sons and two younger daughters, Harold was, as his father had been,
earl of Wessex, the most prominent and prosperous of the jurisdictions
into which England was divided. Next to King Edward, Harold was
England's richest and most powerful man. He was the nation's chief
general and mightiest defender, a valorous soldier, a bold politician
and a capable administrator, distinguished and respected, by many
beloved. He was also brother-in-law to the king, Queen Edith being
his sister.

The point of his departure was likely to have been Bosham Manor,
his home, which had been his father's before him and which stood
overlooking the waters of Chichester harbour, where his private fleet
was based, sheltered in the same coves and inlets that had harboured a
Roman fleet six centuries earlier, when England was still Britannia and
Rome was its master, before the coming of the Anglo-Saxons, Harold's
forebears.

Like most of the other vessels which lay on wooden rollers on the sloping, muddy bank, awaiting their next plunge into the sea, the ship in which Harold would sail was built like a *drakkar*, the longboat of the Vikings, with pointed prow and stern and a lapstrake hull, deckless and exposed to weather and waves, seventy feet or so in length, eighteen feet or so in the beam, propelled by either oars or sail. In its elaborately carved stem and stern-post were iron rings through which its crewmen passed ropes to draw the vessel into and out of the water.

With Harold aboard, the two dozen or more rowers, on the ship-master's command, took to their oars and began driving the ship through the harbour waters, their powerful strokes carrying the vessel out of the creek-fed inlet above which stood Bosham Manor, then past a succession of other inlets and bays, past thatched cottages rising along the reedy shore and huts perched atop stilts at the water's edge. Having entered the harbour's wider waters, the vessel swung south, gliding past the harbour's low-lying sheltering island and into the Solent, the strait leading to the open sea. The crew now shipped their dripping, sixteen-foot-long oars and raised on the vessel's single mast a yard from which draped a square woollen sail, emblazoned with a huge, painted figure of the dragon of Wessex, emblem of the earl of Wessex.

Standing in the bow or in the ship's stern, Harold could watch as, in the distance, the spire of Selsey Cathedral rose on his port side. The landmarks here were familiar to him. As a boy he had learned to sail in these waters off the Isle of Wight and here had been based his father's fleet, which as a young man Harold had commanded. Soon, he knew, the ship would pass within sight of the low bluffs of Selsey Bill and, after that, the Channel proper – and all its perils – would lie dead ahead.

The ship's course was south-south-east from the cape of Selsey Bill. The vessel's helmsman would be steering for a point slightly west of the mouth of the River Seine, a course of deliberate error intended to allow for the effects of the Channel's currents and shifting winds. The ship would be traversing more than seventy miles of open sea, and then would sail into the wide, outstretched arms of the Bay of the Seine. Making about four to four and a half knots, it would take about twenty-two hours to reach the safety of the Seine estuary. More than a third of the voyage would be made in darkness.

As England's second most important person, Harold was, in the minds of many of his countrymen, the best and most logical choice to succeed the ageing, ailing and heirless King Edward. Yet, inexplicably, Harold was the person King Edward had chosen to send to Normandy to solicit a successor. Edward's affinity for Normans, conspicuous since the beginning of his reign, had given England some bad experiences and a bitter bellyful of Normans. Looking across the Channel for someone to reign in England was not a popular move.

Besides, Edward had no right to solicit a successor. Appointing kings was properly the business of the witan, the national council. According to practice, it was the witan that would decide who would be Edward's successor. By soliciting William, Edward was usurping the witan's authority, which was not his only fault.

Neither he nor the nation would have been placed in the position of seeking a successor if Edward, when younger, had done what kings were supposed to do: produce an heir. There would be no impending succession crisis if only Edward had performed like a normal man with his wife and given the nation an atheling, a prince who would have become the rightful and accepted heir to the throne. No one, of course, actually knew what went on – or, perhaps more to the point, *didn't* go on – between Edward and Queen Edith behind closed doors, but there was much speculation. Some guessed that Edward was impotent. Others believed he was a misogynist, perversely affected by his mother's treatment of him as a child. A great many put him down for a homosexual. Many others claimed that he was too exquisitely spiritual to engage in sexual relations of any kind; he was simply above it all.

In any case, his want of an heir had created a crisis that grew greater as the king grew steadily older.

According to traditional accounts, Harold's ship, some hours into its voyage, was overtaken by a storm that came blasting in from the ocean beyond Land's End, its fierce winds driving the ship eastward toward the North Sea.

Finally the storm relented and when daylight returned, Harold and his shipmaster doubtless began looking for a recognisable landmark, something that would identify Cape de la Hève, on the north side of the Bay of the Seine. Around the cape to the south would lie the Seine estuary. Nothing they saw confirmed their hopes, however. They had been swept past the Normandy coast.

Now occurs one of the most critical gaps in the story. What apparently happened was that the ship was beached near the mouth of the

River Somme and Harold and the ship's company were soon captured or fell into a situation in which their capture was imminent.

In all probability Harold was not abjectly defenceless. He was likely to be accompanied by a bodyguard composed of professional soldiers, housecarls. Each would be armed with a broad-bladed, double-edged sword carried in a scabbard at the waist. In one hand each would carry a kite-shaped shield and in the other a lance that could be thrown or thrust with equal deadliness. Over their tunics they wore hauberks, skirted coats of mail that extended below the knees, like metallic nightshirts. The hauberk was slit up to the crotch, front and back, to allow free movement and to protect the legs while on horseback, and most were hooded, the mail hood fitting close to the head and neck and over the chin, leaving only the face, from mouth to eyes, uncovered. Over their mail hoods they wore steel helmets with noseguards.

The ship's crew, who were seafaring soldiers rather than mere sailors, might also be equipped with coats of mail and were likely to be armed like infantry, with swords or long-handled battleaxes and equipped with round shields made of wood and leather. Bodyguard and crew together would have made a small but nevertheless daunting force, unless faced by overwhelming numbers, which they apparently were.

Guy de Ponthieu was count of Ponthieu, the county that lay just beyond Normandy's north-eastern frontier. Guy had become count eleven years earlier, after his brother, Enguerrand, who was leading an army against Duke William of Normandy at the time, had been killed, along with many of his men, in an ambush by William's troops. Enguerrand had picked the wrong side of a fight between William and the French king, Henry I, who, eager to depose William or at least curtail his power, had persuaded a number of counts from northern France to combine forces with his own army and simultaneously attack Normandy from both east and west.

After his brother's death, Guy had quickly taken Enguerrand's place not only as count of Ponthieu but as an ally of King Henry in the continuing campaign against Duke William, which was becoming a losing battle. In February of the next year, 1054, forces loyal to William devastated the armies of Henry's allies in a particularly bloody battle at the town of Mortemer in Normandy. The defeat was so enormous that King Henry lost heart and withdrew from Normandy. Guy managed to avoid being slaughtered with his troops, but became a prisoner of war. In an uncharacteristic act of mercy, William spared Guy. He sent him home and let him remain count of Ponthieu, lord of his own land, but beholden to Duke William, a situation that Guy must have deeply resented.

It seems incredible that Guy would have moved against Harold knowing who he was and discovering that Harold was travelling as the representative of the king of England on a mission to Duke William of Normandy, Guy's overlord. A more reasonable possibility is that Guy managed to corner Harold and his men, *not* knowing that King Edward's personal envoy to the duke of Normandy was his quarry, but soon to find out.

William, the seventh duke of Normandy, was the son of Duke Robert, called Robert the Devil because of his hellish behaviour, which had included summoning to his quarters Arletta the tanner's daughter, who, Bathsheba-like, had provoked his lust while he watched her bathing in a creek near Falaise, a town in western Normandy. William was the result of her response.

Duke Robert died mysteriously (poisoned, some said) in Turkey while on his way home from a pilgrimage to Jerusalem in July 1035. On Robert's death William became duke of Normandy at the age of eight. He also became, and remained throughout his childhood, the target of kidnappers, assassins and other conspirators who coveted his title, wealth and potential power. Those whose own titles, wealth and power depended on the dead duke's heir being preserved in his office protected him, sometimes effecting dramatic rescues at the last minute before the plotters struck.

As a child in 1035 he was warned of a plot to murder him while he was staying in Valognes and he climbed onto a horse in the dead of night and rode through the darkness till he reached Ryes, where he found food and shelter in the home of a peasant family, then rode on to the safety of Falaise. At the Battle of Val-es-Dunes, near Caen, in 1047, as a nineteen-year-old, supported by troops of the French king, William confronted the forces of a group of rebellious barons and boldly charged a renowned knight, driving his sword through the knight's mail and into his breastbone, killing him and, according to the legend, turning the tide of the battle.

Through it all, William developed into a tough and artful survivor, ruthless in putting down challengers, crushing enemies and exacting submission. In the year 1064 he was thirty-six years old, an imposing figure, with a barrel chest, heavy belly, thick arms and strong as a bull, if looks were any indicator.

His grandfather's sister, Emma, had married England's King Aethelred the Unready. Aethelred and Emma became the parents of King Edward. Duke William's father and King Edward's mother were first cousins, making Edward and William cousins once removed.

William had commonly been called the Bastard, even by some of his subjects, but not openly since the affair at Alençon, a town on Normandy's western frontier, where a rebellious crowd taunted him with the word and William, then in his twenties, had his soldiers round up members of the crowd and then had their hands and feet hacked off. After that, the term had fallen into disuse in Normandy.

On a summer day in 1064 Duke William reacted to a new piece of unpleasantness. Somehow Harold or someone acting on Harold's behalf had apparently managed to get word of his predicament past Count Guy's troops and into the ears of someone in Normandy who relayed the news to the duke. A rider on horseback, even an Englishman not familiar with that part of the world, would have been able to follow the Channel coast south-westward until he came to the Normandy border, formed by the River Bresle, perhaps no more than twenty-five miles from the spot where Harold was besieged, or about thirty-five miles from Guy's castle at Beaurain, if indeed Guy had already seized Harold. Across the River Bresle, on the south bank, the rider would find the city of Eu, a Norman stronghold. From there a courier would be quickly dispatched to report the alarming news to William.

William apparently was outraged. He sent word demanding that Guy hand over Harold and his men inside Norman territory, probably to make certain that it was Count Guy himself who safely escorted the Englishmen out of Ponthieu. William chose Eu as the place where Harold would be turned over to him.

Eu was the nearest Norman city and it had another significance. It was the citadel of Robert, count of Eu, one of the duke's most powerful supporters and his cousin as well. Robert's father and William's grandfather, Duke Richard II, were brothers. It was Robert of Eu who, with his army, had caught the French king's forces by surprise and inflicted on them the overwhelming defeat at Mortemer. That was when Robert's soldiers had taken Count Guy prisoner, and Robert then had turned Guy over to the duke.

The duke and Count Robert were close. Fourteen years earlier, when William married tiny Matilda, daughter of the count of Flanders, Robert had hosted the wedding ceremony and the festivities in his grand old castle at Eu, set like a brilliant jewel in a lush private park, surrounded by magnificent beech trees and overlooking the winding River Bresle as it coursed through that ancient city near the sea.

William, with an armed troop of cavalry, went himself to receive Harold when Guy turned him over. Guy had a valid case to make to the duke. Under the law, Guy was entitled to collect a forfeit – very much like a ransom – when seafarers were shipwrecked on his shores. William recognised Guy's right. A ship need not be ruined, even disabled, for it to be considered a shipwreck under the law. Merely being forced ashore in a storm was enough. Among the unknown facts is whether ransom was paid to Guy and, if so, by whom – Harold or William? It is probable that it was paid and that William paid it. In any event – but particularly if William had ransomed him – Harold, doubtless with a keen sense of medieval honour, now felt obligated to William, despite an intense dislike for him as the prince of Normans and as Edward's choice as his successor.

Once the business with Guy was done, William would eventually get around to discovering from Harold what King Edward's message to him was. Harold would likely report on the king's health, telling the duke that Edward was well but not so strong, and he would also tell William that Edward had sent him to put a question to the duke. King Edward would like to discover the depth of the duke's interest in succeeding to the throne of England. William perhaps was surprised. Edward had, according to William, already promised him the throne, some thirteen years earlier. He informed Harold that he, William, had accepted Edward's promise then and that he was holding Edward to it now. As far as he was concerned, his succession to England's throne was, in the language of the Normans, *un fait accompli*.

2

THE PROPOSITION
SUMMER 1064

O nce a Gaullish settlement named Ratuma and later the Roman city Rotomagus, Rouen was more than nine and a half centuries old in 911 when the cunning Viking chieftain Rolf, or Rollo as the French called him, inveigled the French king, Charles the Simple, into officially ceding to him what he and his Viking followers already possessed. It was that part of French territory that had been Neustria, which at the historic moment of its cession to Rollo became the new duchy of Normandy. Rollo thus became the first duke of Normandy, and Rouen, sitting sedately astride the River Seine as it snaked its way from Paris to the sea, became Duke Rollo's capital city.

It was to Rouen that Duke William, the great-great-great-grandson of Duke Rollo, took Earl Harold. During the next few days William kept Harold entertained. One evening he gave a *soirée* for Harold in the palace, an occasion for Harold to meet William's closest associates. The guest list probably included the duke's two half-brothers, born to William's mother, Arletta, after Duke Robert had tired of her and had given her as a wife to Herluin, the viscount of Conteville. One brother was Odo, who was, by William's appointment, bishop of Bayeux. The other was Robert, count of Mortain.

Also attending would probably be William fitz Osbern, the duke's seneschal and oldest friend, and a distant relative as well. His father,

Osbern, had been seneschal to Duke William's father and a guardian of the duke as a young child. William fitz Osbern was also lord of Breteuil.

Others likely to have been there were the duke's cousin Richard of Evreux, Roger of Montgomery, Roger of Beaumont, the young Hugh of Montford, the young Walter Giffard, Hugh of Grandmesnil, Hugh of Avranches, William of Warenne, and Ralph of Toesni, William fitz Osbern's brother-in-law. Another likely guest would be John of Ravenna, the duke's nephew and head of the abbey in the city of Fécamp, on the Normandy coast. Harold knew about the abbey. King Edward, in his love of God and all things Norman, had given the abbey several Sussex seaports as a perpetual endowment, making them, in effect, pieces of Normandy on English soil, an arrangement that rankled English patriots. There would also be William of Poitiers, a soldier turned cleric, a man with a gift for words and public relations.

The *soirée* may have been the occasion at which Duke William made Harold a momentous proposition. Confiding to Harold that he, William, needed someone to watch out for his interests in England, he proposed that the two of them, he and Earl Harold, should have an agreement. The agreement would be made in realisation that the death of a king who had no heir could cause an unstable situation, and that he and Harold both had much to lose in such a situation.

What he wanted, William made clear, was for him and Harold to agree that while Edward still lived, Harold would protect William's interests at Edward's court. In return, William would protect Harold's interests when Edward was no longer king. Edward's death, William assured Harold, would not affect Harold's earldom nor diminish any of his powers or interests. William promised to guarantee Harold's position and his property.

To seal their agreement and bind themselves to each other, the duke offered to give Harold his daughter Agatha in marriage. That would make them – Harold and William – family, kinsmen.

Harold, however, already had a wife. To all intents and purposes, Edith Swan's Neck, the mother of his five children, was his wife, although she was a handfast wife. Theirs was, in the term of the times, a Danish marriage. There had not been a wedding ceremony, neither had the marriage been sanctioned by the Church. Actually, it wasn't anything unusual; such marriages were common in England.

If Harold asked about the age of William's daughter, doubting that he had a child of marriageable age, he would have learned that she was twelve years old. It would be an obviously political marriage. William's idea was to have Harold agree to the marriage for the present and plan it for the future.

Before Harold could decently take his leave from Normandy and from William, more unpleasant news came to the duke.

Conan, count of Brittany, had laid siege to Dol, a Breton town about twelve miles west of the River Couesnon, which formed part of the boundary that separated Normandy and Brittany. Riwallon, lord of Dol, was surrounded, unable to break through the siege and soon to run out of food. The situation was desperate.

William regarded Conan as a dangerous irritant, a man who nurtured a belief – not without merit – that Normandy should be his, not William's, and that one day he would wrest it from William. It was in William's interest to support Riwallon in his rebellion against Conan.

William invited Harold to come with him to Dol, knowing Harold's reputation as a general. It is probable that Harold didn't want to get involved, but also probable that he was thinking that a refusal would seem, at best, ungrateful. At worst, it could be seen as fear or hostility. Weighing his choices, he apparently saw little harm in going, but a great deal of possible harm in not going. In any case, he agreed to go with William.

The duke doubtless ordered out a force of several battalions, including cavalry, infantry and archers, and gave a short deadline for the troops to march.

Brittany was a French county once known as Armorica, a Romanisation of the Celtic words for 'seaside'. It had been renamed for its inhabitants, the Celtic Britons (or Bretons, in French), the same people who had moved *en masse* to inhabit the British Isles that lay across the English Channel. The renaming had been done by the Franks, a people who in the early Middle Ages had swept in from the regions around the Rhine River and had overrun the Celts and established the empire that was to become France. The Celts of Brittany, however, had never been assimilated by the Franks, and their land, a peninsula at the north-western tip of Europe, bounded by the English Channel on the north, the Atlantic Ocean on the west and the Bay of

Biscay on the south, continued to exist quaintly as the last remaining Celtic stronghold on the Continent.

The route that Duke William chose for the march from Rouen to Dol led westward through Caen, then south-west to Avranches, south across the River Sélune, west along the coast of the Bay of Mont St Michel, across the estuary of the Couesnon, then south again at a point north-west of Pontorson and on to Dol.

William was likely to have sent a company of cavalry ahead of the main body of his force to serve as an advance guard. About a mile and a half to the rear of the advance guard would ride the duke himself, at the head of a long column of horses and men that filled the roadway from one side to the other, moving steadily while curious peasants and villagers gawped at the spectacle from fields and houses beside the road.

Harold probably rode beside the duke, and behind Harold came the soldiers of Harold's bodyguard. Behind them would come William's battalions of cavalry, armed with lances and swords, and mounted infantry who, when the time for battle arrived, would dismount to fight on foot with sword, axe or mace. Behind them came a company of archers, also mounted until the battle was about to be joined. A company of cavalry rode at the end of the column as a rearguard.

As he rode, William carried a mace in his right hand and held his horse's reins in his left. Harold carried a lance in his right hand and a kite-shaped shield emblazoned with the dragon of Wessex in his left, with which he also held the reins.

The specifics of what happened next are unrecorded. To recreate the drama of it requires conjecture. Perhaps the action happened like this: shortly after dawn on the morning of the fourth day of the march, as the sun strove to dissolve low-lying, misty clouds of fog along the shoreline of the Bay of Mont St Michel, the men riding point in Duke William's advance guard drew up their mounts at the edge of the River Couesnon. They paused warily at the water's edge, preparing to ford the shoals near the river's mouth. Off to their right, within their sight, rose the mystical Mont St Michel, the granite island on which Duke William's great-grandfather, Duke Richard I, had built a Benedictine monastery.

The shallow water and shifting sands of the river bottom here looked safe enough, but the veterans among the chevaliers of William's advance guard knew the treachery of the Couesnon shoals. For the reckless or luckless there were pools of quicksand lying in wait, and a misstep by man or mount could mean agonising death.

The chevaliers entered the water slowly, perhaps in single file. After several tense minutes, the point men were safely across the river, and the remainder of the advance guard drew up at the riverbank and prepared to cross also. The riders were crossing with their eyes fixed on the point men on the far shore, keeping their mounts lined up with them so as not to drift from the safe path through the shoals.

The crossing was slow, and by the time the riders at the rear of the advance guard entered the water, Duke William and Earl Harold, at the head of the force's main body, were within sight of the river's edge. Suddenly a horse near midstream balked and stumbled and its rider fell from its back and plunged into the river, which instantly carried him seaward. As he thrashed about, trying to gain his footing in the waist-high water, he stepped into a pool of quicksand, which instantly began drawing him down. The efforts of his comrades to save him resulted in their being trapped in the quicksand also.

Risking his own life, Harold impulsively raced toward the sinking soldiers. Without more details, it's difficult to picture how the rescue was effected, but Harold somehow managed to get the Norman soldiers and himself safely out of the quicksand and the river.

What is easier to imagine is Duke William sitting astride his horse and watching the drama with astonishment, impressed by Harold's courage, more so by his rashness.

The town of Dol was a collection of houses and shops above which rose the town's two dominant structures, the stone church and Riwallon's castle. The castle, which crowned a hillock near the centre of the town, was a wooden structure at the centre of an earthworks fortification that was surrounded by a tall wooden stockade. Outside the stockade was a moat crossed by a drawbridge.

When he was within a few miles of Dol, William began collecting useful intelligence from peasants and travellers. He learned that Count Conan's troops had burned many of the town's buildings, forcing the townspeople to flee into the earthworks fortification. Conan had not made an assault on the fortification. He was maintaining a ring of troops around it, intending to starve Riwallon into surrender.

Before William could manoeuvre his troops and fall upon Conan's army with his full force, Conan, apparently warned of William's approach, quickly abandoned his siege and hurriedly fled south toward Rennes, Brittany's capital city, thirty miles due south of Dol.

Apparently not wishing to engage Conan's army unnecessarily, William decided against pursuing it. After some time spent at Dol, he reformed his columns and marched on Dinan, a Breton town on the River Rance, about fifteen miles south-west of Dol. His objective is not now clear, but perhaps it was to inflict a punishment on Conan for the siege of Dol and the threat against Riwallon.

Dinan's main fortification was a wooden fortress, encircled by a wooden palisade, overlooking the River Rance. There, faced with an imminent assault by William's army, the town's defenders assembled to make a stand. William, however, had no intention either of enduring a lengthy siege or of hurling his men at the fortress walls. Once more there are gaps in the details, but reasonable speculation fills them in. In iron braziers set up across from the west, south and east faces of the fortress palisade, Duke William's archers built small fires. Beside the braziers they laid bundles of arrows, the tips of their shafts coated with a thin layer of pitch. Now they stood with bows in hand, awaiting the command of their captain.

William signalled the captain, and soon flaming arrows were arching through the sky, raining fire upon the wooden fortification. From within the fortress came the alarms of the Breton defenders, then the sounds of panic as the burning arrows stabbed the fortress timbers repeatedly with flame. Within minutes the entire fortress was alight and tall spikes of flame and pillars of smoke were rising into the sky.

After many minutes, cries came from atop the palisade. The defenders were shouting their surrender. The gates opened, and the Breton defenders started streaming out, to be immediately surrounded by the mass of William's infantry that grimly encircled the fortress walls. The Norman infantrymen seized the arms and armour of the Bretons as they rushed out to escape the flames.

A formal surrender followed, with the keys of the city literally handed over to the duke. Apparently satisfied, William within days reassembled his battalions and marched back to Rouen.

3
THE UNINTENDED OATH
SUMMER 1064

Following the return of Harold and William to Rouen, there occurred the most momentous event of Harold's Normandy mission, the culmination of its history-shaping incidents. The exact circumstances are unrecorded, but the significant facts are known. What is to be conjectured is a cavernous great hall in the duke's palace at Rouen, with William sitting at the head of a long table laden with food and drink. Down either side of the table, beginning with William fitz Osbern on the duke's right and his half-brother Odo the bishop on his left, sit the duke's audience, a large assembly of friends and vassals, many of whom Harold had met at the last large social occasion in the palace. This time the guests had gathered to welcome the duke home and celebrate his victory. At the far end of the table, perhaps, sit Harold and his translator.

The duke rises to make a toast. He looks down the long table and meets Harold's eyes, then raises his cup. All the guests stand with William as he speaks, saluting Harold. All lift their cups and shout in unison their toast to Earl Harold. They then drink with the duke. When his cup is emptied, William puts it down and gives a signal. A swarm of attendants quickly steps to the table and removes platters and bowls, plates and cups, soiled towels, all the remains of the banquet, then files out of the room.

Now there is a ceremony. Several monks, perhaps, at this point enter the chamber bearing two reliquaries and a portable altar. They place the altar on the table, facing the duke. The reliquaries are placed nearby on the table.

The duke commands Harold to come forward.

Hesitatingly, Harold pushes back from the table, stands and begins walking toward William at the far end of the table, motioning for his translator to come along with him.

As Harold stands before him, the duke delivers a speech. He says something to the effect that from this day forward Earl Harold is to enjoy every privilege that the duke can grant a nobleman of Normandy. He says that the earl of Wessex has this day entered into the protection of the duke of Normandy.

William then places his hands upon the two reliquaries and holds them there. He asks Harold to do the same, which Harold does. Then the duke says something like this:

> With all due solemnity, I, William, duke of Normandy, do hereby swear before Almighty God and this honourable company and on these sacred relics, the holy, mortal remains of God's Saints Rasyphus and Ravennus, that Harold, earl of Wessex, is by his valour, my will and this holy act a knight of the duchy of Normandy.

While his and Harold's hands remain on the reliquaries, William asks Harold if he, before God and the assembled company and on these holy relics, does truly accept this knighthood.

Whatever acceptance of Norman knighthood might entail, and perhaps he wasn't quite sure what it meant for him, Harold apparently hastily decided that under the circumstances it would be a bigger mistake to refuse it than to accept it.

He accepted.

The ceremony would then have continued. William perhaps now signalled to three courtiers to file in and stand beside him. One held a lance bearing a Norman gonfalon below the lancepoint. The second held a Norman sword in a leather scabbard, and the third one held a conical, steel-and-leather Norman helmet, new and gleaming.

William took the helmet in both hands and placed it on Harold's head. He then took the sword and handed it to Harold, then the lance. While Harold stood holding the Norman arms, sword in one hand, lance in the other, William raised his right hand and shouted, 'Long live

Earl Harold, liegeman of Normandy!'

The seated Normans scrambled to their feet and shouted back, 'Long live Earl Harold, liegeman of Normandy!'

It had been the devil's own mission from the very beginning – the mission he didn't want but couldn't refuse, the storm that had carried him to Ponthieu's shore, the capture or imminent capture by Count Guy, the rescue that had led to his indebtedness to William, and now this damnable unforeseen development. If he reflected on the chain of unfortunate events that had brought him to this unhappy pass, Harold might have begun to wonder if the turn of events could be the effect of a curse he bore.

Vivid in his mind would be the haunting memory of the night that his father, the late Earl Godwin, had been stricken. On Easter Monday in 1053, King Edward had thrown a huge banquet in the palace at Winchester, and Earl Godwin, then about sixty-five years old, was one of the obligatory invitees. Near the end of the meal Edward, his passion inflamed by drink, stood up from his seat on the dais and, within the hearing of everyone in the hall, angrily accused Godwin of the murder of Edward's younger brother, Prince Alfred, who had had his eyes gouged out by order of King Canute and had died of the trauma.

'By God', Godwin swore loudly before the entire group of guests, 'I am innocent!' He pounded the table with his big fist and shouted, food falling from his mouth, 'I swear I'm guiltless of Prince Alfred's death! May God strike me dead if I'm lying!'

At that his face turned florid and he clutched his throat. Then he pitched forward, his head falling face first into his plate. Four days later he was dead, having never regained consciousness.

Harold had been sitting beside him, and he and his brothers Tostig and Gyrth had lifted Godwin unconscious from the table and carried him to King Edward's chambers, where the king had said to take him. As they carried him, Harold could see his father's face, his mouth open, his eyes staring, as if he had suddenly confronted a sight so terrifying that it had ripped the heart from him.

Earl Godwin was not someone easily frightened, by man or God, which was all the more reason he could swear as he had done so readily. Had God on that Easter Monday night shown Godwin, before Harold and all those other witnesses, that He does not take such oaths lightly? In the more credulous eleventh century, one – including Earl Harold –

could easily believe so. Still more frightening to him was the nagging possibility that God's punishment had not ended with the life of Godwin, but that the sins of the father were to be visited upon the sons.

The advice of Harold's old comrades-in-arms, those confidants of his who served him in his bodyguard and who gathered with him in his quarters in Duke William's castle, would be that he should put thoughts of a curse out of his head. The menace Harold faced, they perhaps pointed out, was Duke William, not God's vengeance. Harold would be advised to forget, too, that ceremony staged by the Bastard. Harold had sworn under duress, and no one, God Himself not excepted, could reasonably expect a man to keep an oath not freely made.

His own best advice or that of his confidants would have been to tell the Bastard whatever he wanted to hear, then clear the hell out of Normandy. Everything, Harold realised, would look very much different once he was back in England.

In a new meeting soon after the knighting the duke emphasised that he wanted Harold to represent him at the court of King Edward and to keep his interests before the king and his advisors. He said that upon King Edward's death, he wanted Harold to present William's claim to the throne to the witan and press for its acceptance. In the meantime, the duke said, Harold would arrange to have a battalion of Norman troops garrisoned in Dover; Harold would keep them provisioned and under his protection.

In return for those great favours, the duke said, he guaranteed Harold all the authority and privileges, all the titles, lands and other property that he now possessed. William promised to Harold and his family all the protection that William's powers could provide. In addition, he would give Harold his gratitude and his steadfast friendship, now and forever.

Besides all that, William said, he would give Harold his daughter Agatha to wed, to bind their families together. They would work out the details of the marriage ceremony later. And to strengthen their ties even further, William said, he would very much like Harold to give his younger sister to one of William's nobles to be his wife.

When Harold agreed, the duke, in one way or another, told Harold, 'Well done. We have a bargain.'

Shortly after that – with a boatload of gifts for Harold and his family, and gifts for King Edward and his queen – Harold and his men sailed at last for England and home.

4
THE KING
SUMMER 1064

At the end of the tenth century Danish Vikings terrorised England's coastal towns as they had done in the eighth and ninth centuries. Swarming out of their longboats, they overwhelmed the towns' defenders, slaughtering them with sword and axe until the towns fell helpless. They pillaged whatever could be carried off and, as survivors of the onslaught helplessly watched, they publicly raped the women, lining up to take turns ravishing wives, daughters and mothers. The young people of the towns were rounded up and herded down to the longboats to be hauled off and sold into slavery. Finally the marauders set fire to the towns and sailed away, leaving nought but despair and devastation in their wake.

Aethelred, who was England's king then, eventually came up with a strategy for combating the Viking menace. The Normans, themselves descendants of Vikings, frequently showed their affinity for them by offering their ports to England's tormentors, providing them with bases from which to launch their raids. Aethelred decided to eliminate that advantage. In 991 he signed a treaty with Duke Richard of Normandy to bar Danish raiders from Norman ports. England and Normandy became linked.

Eleven years later, in 1002, King Aethelred strengthened the link. He married Emma, sister of the then ruling duke of Normandy, Richard

II, who was the father of Robert the Devil. When Aethelred died in 1016, he left four sons. Two were sons by Emma: Edward and Alfred. Two were by his discarded first wife: Edmund Ironside and Eadwig. Edmund Ironside claimed the crown on his father's death but wasn't strong enough to hold it against the aggressive and determined Danish prince, Canute.

Canute commanded a large following in England, most of his supporters being Danes whose forebears had settled in England during the great Danish Viking incursions in the eighth and ninth centuries. With strong support from the Danish English, and many Saxon English as well, Canute proclaimed himself king of England. Edward and Alfred, the last remaining legitimate and Saxon heirs to the throne, escaped with their mother and took refuge in the protective arms of their Norman relatives.

In a bizarre turn of events, Canute, wishing to legitimise his accession to the English throne and to create an alliance with Normandy, a strategic must, offered to marry Emma, the widowed former queen. Emma accepted his proposal. In July 1017 she left young Edward and Alfred in Normandy and sailed back to England to become queen once more.

Edward remained in Normandy, succoured by his Norman kin and their friends. He owed them for their hospitality; more than that, he owed them for his life.

On Canute's death in 1035, the crown passed first to Harold Harefoot, Canute's son by his first wife, then three years later, when Harold Harefoot died, to Harthacanute, Canute's son by Emma and thus the half-brother of Edward. On Harthacanute's death in 1042, the crown came at last to Edward, recalled from Normandy to a country that after an absence of twenty-seven years no longer seemed like home.

By the grace of God still king of England in 1064, at age sixty, Edward was showing signs of failing health. Upon Harold's return, Edward received him in the Westminster palace and invited Harold to give a complete report of his mission to Duke William. Doubtless Harold left out a lot, saying nothing about his knighting by William, or about the oath, or about his agreements with William.

At that same meeting or one held shortly thereafter, Edward broached a new subject with Harold, one that had become increasingly troubling to him and dangerous to the country. England had an extremely serious problem, Edward confided earnestly to Harold. The problem, he declared, was Tostig Godwinson, earl of Northumbria and younger brother of Harold. Something, the king said, had to be done about Tostig. And it had to be done immediately.

Edward had appointed Tostig earl of Northumbria in 1055, following the death of Earl Siward. At making war, Tostig was the equal of Harold. That was perhaps the chief quality that Edward was looking for when he appointed Tostig earl. Northumbria was vital to the defence of England, situated as it was on the North Sea, opposite Norway, and on the border of Scotland. Edward wanted a strong military leader in charge there.

As a general, Tostig had served Edward well enough, particularly in the elimination of the king of Wales, Griffith ap Llewellyn, as a threat to the western shires. In ways other than military, however, Tostig had disappointed Edward, and as autumn approached in 1064, the king's disappointment was reaching a critical stage.

Edward now let Harold know that he believed he had made a mistake in giving Northumbria to Tostig. Edward probably felt that Harold should share the blame for his mistake, since Harold had played a large part in the appointment. He and Queen Edith had both urged Edward to appoint Tostig.

Edward explained the problem. His explanation would have been something like this: Tostig had done what he thought was right, but it was wrong in Northumbria. Northumbrians were not like the people of Wessex. They were a different breed. They were more independent and more stubborn – perhaps because of their Viking blood. Tostig's sense of justice and his harshness were offensive to Northumbrians. They resented him. They also resented his being a West Saxon. They resented having a Godwinson as earl of Northumbria.

Harold would have understood that part of Edward's explanation and accepted it. Northumbrians were both jealous and fearful of the wealth and power of the Godwinson brothers, four of whom – Harold, Tostig, Gyrth and Leofwine – were earls, together controlling three quarters of England.

Royal informants were reporting to Edward that there was talk of rebellion against Tostig. Some thanes were for him, but many more were strongly opposed. Harold knew as well as Edward that a unified

Northumbria, under a strong leader, was essential to England's security. Northumbria offered some of the likeliest points of attack for a Norse invasion, and the threat of one was real. King Harald Hardrada of Norway was insisting that he had a right to the English throne. What was more, he had a history of settling disputes, successfully, by force of arms.

Besides the potential danger from Hardrada there was the smouldering enmity of the Scots toward the English. The king of the Scots, Malcolm Canmore, although paying lip-service allegiance to Edward, had never been a willing subordinate of the English king. He was a man who bore watching, occupying, as he did, the rugged lands beyond the northern frontier of Northumbria and of England.

Edward apparently emphasised to Harold that something had to be done about Tostig. He must be made to change his ways. He must be made to see that people in Northumbria were deeply troubled by his methods. He must be made to see the necessity of adapting his ways to the ways of the Northumbrians.

Edward had decided that Harold should go and talk to Tostig, in the dim hope that he could and would change.

Harold likely protested the assignment, asking Edward if it wouldn't be better done by the king himself. To that question Edward would have replied that he had already spoken to Tostig about the problem and that Tostig had told him that he, Edward, was too easygoing and that a firm hand was what was needed in Northumbria.

Harold may have made another attempt to avoid the task, reminding Edward that Queen Edith was close to Tostig and suggesting she should be the one to talk to him.

Edward would turn aside that suggestion as well, complaining that Edith always took Tostig's side, that she was *too* close to him. It was Harold, Edward insisted, who must talk to Tostig. The matter was too important for Harold to shirk the task.

5
THE REBELLION
SUMMER 1064–AUTUMN 1065

From Westminster Harold likely set out first for Bosham. He doubtless was yearning for Edith Swan's Neck and was eager to see the children. There were three boys – Godwin, about eighteen, named for Harold's father; Edmund, about seventeen; and Magnus, about fifteen – and two younger girls, Gunhild and Gytha, both probably under twelve. When she was a girl, Edith, now around forty, had gained her nickname, Swan's Neck, from the graceful creature of which her admirers were apparently reminded when they gazed upon her.

Following dinner and some time with the children, Harold and Edith would retire to the privacy of their bedroom. Later perhaps they would lie together and talk, of Normandy and other things, and as he spoke perhaps her finger lightly traced on his shoulder or chest an old battle scar, one that would become important in the days ahead. Edith may not have heard about the outrage that had moved King Edward to dispatch Harold on the mission to Tostig, and Harold might have talked about it, telling her what he had learned from Edward and explaining why he would be leaving Bosham shortly.

The scandal concerned two young thanes of Northumbria, Gamal Ormson and Ulf Dolfinson, whom Tostig had invited to his estate in an effort to win their loyalty. He promised their fathers, who were not among his supporters, that he would guarantee their safety. But when his blandishments and implicit bribes failed to win over the young men, an angry argument ensued and Tostig erupted in a rage that resulted in his having them murdered at his manor in York.

Northumbria had erupted in angry protests, and the situation was threatening to become worse. One night with Edith may have been all that Harold could have afforded to spend before he hurried off to try to restore calm and retrieve order in Northumbria. And so, not long after his arrival at Bosham, he was off again.

The trip to Northumbria was a rare one for Harold. He seldom travelled into England's north country, the part of England known as the Danelaw, a region where the population was heavily weighted by Danes whose Viking forebears in the ninth century had come in hordes, first as marauders, then as settlers. They had wrested the land from the Anglo-Saxons and had imposed their own justice, their own traditions and, for a time, their own religion, language and politics. They were northerners, provincial and wary of southerners, and particularly wary of powerful southerners such as the Godwinsons.

The political, commercial and ecclesiastical capital of Northumbria was York, which had a population of more than 8,000 souls, making it England's third largest city, ranking behind London and Winchester. There the Northumbrian witan – composed of thanes, leading citizens and ranking churchmen – held their gemot, their council meeting. There, to satisfy the city's commercial needs, ten mints operated, striking coins under licence from the king. There also was the seat of the archbishop of York, overseer of one of England's two archdioceses, the other one being the archdiocese of Canterbury. There, too, was the official residence of the earl of Northumbria, Tostig Godwinson, though he spent more time in London than in York.

With his bodyguard, Harold approached York from the south-west, crossed the River Ouse and entered through the heavily guarded south gate of the walled city. He proceeded straight to the market square, past the cathedral and on to the public hall, where he would meet with Tostig.

The meeting did not go well. Harold's delivery of the king's message, cloaked with as much tact as Harold could manage, which was apparently less than needed, offended Tostig, sensitive as he was to criticism, particularly coming from the brother he considered a rival.

If provoked by Tostig, Harold was likely to have spelt out Edward's specific complaints: Tostig had imposed taxes and fines that people found unbearable; he often acted out of anger rather than reason; he was too inflexible in his dealings with the Northumbrians; he lacked pity; he tended toward self-righteousness, unable to see when the fault was his.

If these were laid out to him, Tostig may well have heard the criticisms as Harold's, not necessarily Edward's, which would have set off an acrimonious reaction. In any case, the meeting evidently ended without having accomplished anything even faintly resembling what King Edward had intended. Instead, it had served only to drive a wedge between the brothers, the first step in Tostig's complete and bitter alienation from Harold.

Godwin's daughter Edith, who had long since despaired of bearing a child by King Edward, had settled into the role Edward had apparently intended for her from the beginning. She was the king's companion or, as he liked to say, his daughter. By his choice, she did not serve as his wife.

Now past forty-five, Queen Edith had turned from a lovely girl into a handsome woman. Aside from her husband the king, to whom she had become obviously devoted, her closest friend was her brother Tostig, to whom she had been a protective older sister ever since he was a small boy. He was a frequent guest at court and in the king and queen's private chambers. Edith could respect her brother Harold, but Tostig – charming until provoked, handsome, effervescent – she adored.

As Christmas 1064 neared, Tostig's troubles with the Northumbrian noblemen continued to mount. One thane was especially bothersome to him. He was Gospatric, a young man with a temper as fiery as Tostig's and a gift for inflammatory oratory, which became more impassioned and seditious with ale and a sympathetic audience of other disgruntled thanes. After the murders of Gamal and Ulf, however, and the storm of reaction that followed and still had not subsided, Tostig was disinclined to move directly against Gospatric, despite an enormous desire to do so.

While Tostig and his wife, Judith, and their children were guests in the Westminster palace at Christmas time, Tostig evidently went to Queen Edith and asked her for a favour. He told her about Gospatric.

He wanted to get rid of him, but discreetly, in a way that would not have people immediately suspecting him. Edith evidently said she would help.

Three days after Christmas, Gospatric, a newly invited guest at the palace, was lured into a fight and was stabbed to death in the royal court. Northumbrians immediately blamed Tostig.

Edward's choice of Tostig as earl in 1055 was unpopular among Northumbrians from the beginning. As time went on, they found him not merely unacceptable but increasingly unbearable. On 3 October 1065, after ten years of his rule and with murders of the three young thanes still fresh in the minds, the Northumbrians took action while Tostig was off hunting with King Edward in Wiltshire.

An army of rebellious thanes, their numbers in the hundreds, marched on York and invaded Tostig's residence, quickly overcoming and virtually wiping out Tostig's loyal housecarls and retainers. Only a few managed to escape, including Copsig, Tostig's deputy, who ran things while Tostig was away, which was often. The rebels broke into the treasury and the armoury and took everything. They called the Northumbrian witan into a gemot, an official assembly, in the public hall in York and by their own authority stripped Tostig of his title, property and power, and declared him an outlaw. They then sent for Morkere, brother of Earl Edwin of Mercia, to make him the new earl of Northumbria.

By the time news of the rebellion reached Tostig and Edward at the king's hunting pavilion in Wiltshire, the rebel army was marching south through Northumbria behind Morkere, slaughtering Tostig's adherents and seizing his lands as it drove toward Lincoln and Nottingham, in Mercia, gathering recruits and strength as it went.

Mercia was the earldom lying to the south of Northumbria, in England's Midlands. During the time of King Canute and until 1057 it had been ruled by Earl Leofric, member of a distinguished Mercian family (and perhaps best known to history as the husband of the enchanting Lady Godiva). In controversial matters Leofric tended to side with his Northumbrian neighbours. Like Northumbrians, Mercians were suspicious and resentful of West Saxons generally and the Godwin family members in particular. Following Leofric's death in 1057, he was succeeded by his son, Aelfgar, an erratic and self-destructive man who, in the royal court two years earlier, had contested Tostig for the earldom of Northumbria and had thereby begun a bitter feud with Tostig. Although he sometimes obviously gave no care to offending King Edward, Aelfgar wanted so eagerly to gain King Griffith's favour that he gave the Welsh king his daughter, Alditha, for a wife and made a pact with him, apart from Edward's policy toward Griffith.

For that and other acts considered by Edward to be seditious, and probably at the urging of Tostig, who hated him, Aelfgar was stripped of his position as earl of Mercia and expelled from the country by order of King Edward. In 1062 the elder of Aelfgar's two sons, Edwin, then a teenager, was appointed by King Edward to be earl of Mercia. Both Edwin and his brother, Morkere, had grown up hearing their father's vitriolic rantings against Tostig, whom Aelfgar blamed for every wrong done him by King Edward, and their resentment toward Tostig had been long simmering. Now, with a powerful rebel force behind them, the brothers Edwin and Morkere were at last in a position to take their vengeance against Tostig, and possibly against Edward, if he should decide to stand in their way.

Upon hearing of the rebellion, Edward immediately sent couriers from Wiltshire to summon his counsellors to an emergency meeting to be held in Britford, not far from where he had been hunting. Harold was among them. What Edward had feared *could* happen *had* happened, and he would make that point to Harold. But what he had not expected was the Northumbrian thanes going so far as to usurp the king's authority and directly challenge him. In so doing, the way Edward saw it, the Northumbrians had committed treason.

Harold's question to Edward now would be: What exactly do the Northumbrians want and what do they intend? If he asked Edward whether the Northumbrians had sent word to him, Edward's response would have been that they had not. Harold also might have asked how it was that the king, whose poor health was obvious, was out hunting. Edward would have admitted that he was there because of Tostig. Tostig had urged him to go hunting with him, as he had done frequently in the past, Tostig being one of Edward's favourite hunting companions. But at the hunt, hunting was only part of Tostig's activity. He had been practically haranguing Edward, defending his actions in Northumbria and urging Edward to trust him.

Upon the arrival of the king's other advisors, Edward convened the meeting. Not all the details of the meeting are known, but some of them may be deduced. Not all members of the witan were there, but many were: the earls, not including Edwin of Mercia; some of the leading thanes; several bishops; a few court officials. Tostig, too, was there. When he and Harold met again, it was likely to have been an awkward moment.

By now the king had received new intelligence on the Northumbrian thanes; he knew that they had declared Morkere to be their earl to replace Tostig and behind Morkere they were proceeding toward Northampton, their ranks swelled immensely by the addition of Earl Edwin's Mercian army, including Edwin himself, plus a sizable contingent of Welsh fighting men. They were now a force to be reckoned with, even by the king. The king's counsellors were briefed on the situation, and their advice was solicited.

Someone among the king's counsellors – but not Harold – may well have taken the opportunity to condemn Tostig for his years of misrule. His harsh measures, his abrogation of the traditional laws of the Danes, his despoliation of Church properties, his mean-spiritedness and lack of mercy – all those things together had caused the men of Northumbria to act. The blame for what was happening was Tostig's, not the Northumbrian rebels'.

Tostig would have made a strong protest. In his mind it was Harold who was responsible. Harold, he now believed, had conspired with the Northumbrian thanes and evoked the rebellion purposely to drive Tostig from power.

Finally the king's counsellors agreed that Edward should send someone to parley with the rebels, to hear their grievances and demands, bear to them the king's reasonable responses and try to reach a compromise. No one, with the exception of Tostig, wanted an armed confrontation. A civil war must be averted if at all possible.

Harold was the man King Edward chose to hear the rebels and speak for him.

Bearing the king's standards, the column of Harold's housecarls, with Harold at its head, advanced toward Northampton from the south. Along the road, from the hour that the column entered Mercia, Mercian spies were doubtlessly following the progress of the Wessexmen and by the time Harold and his troops neared the gates of Northampton, details of Mercian soldiers were standing guard outside the city, awaiting the king's representative.

Harold was escorted into the presence of the Northumbrian and Mercian leaders. Morkere, the rebels' new earl of Northumbria, a young man, perhaps no more than twenty years old, may have been first to greet him. Harold likely recognised him and cordially returned his greeting. Harold made it clear that he had come in the name of the king and that the words he brought were the king's words. He would be acting for King Edward, not himself.

Edwin, earl of Mercia, probably a couple of years older than his brother, would also have been there, as well as leaders of the Northumbrian thanes' conspiracy. Whoever spoke for the Northumbrian thanes would be likely to declare the causes of their rebellion and defend what they had done. They would tell Harold that they in gemot had removed Tostig from his former position and had appointed Morkere Aelfgarson to be the new earl of Northumbria. They would tell him that all lands and other property formerly belonging to Tostig had been confiscated. And they would tell him that Tostig, for his crimes and other offences, had been declared by the Northumbrian witanagemot to be an outlaw and subject to all appropriate penalties if apprehended.

Harold, voicing the king's objection, would tell the men of Northumbria that they had taken those actions without resort to the king and without the benefit of the king's advice.

The Northumbrian spokesman would reply that all that they did was necessary and that the need for their actions was urgent. Then he told Harold that they wanted the king to confirm the actions of their witanagemot.

Harold responded, saying that the king had sent him to assure the Northumbrians that he would listen to all their grievances and hear them with sympathy. The king would make whatever changes were necessary to regain peace and the good will of Northumbrians under the rule of Earl Tostig. The king stood ready to compromise with the men of Northumbria.

The Northumbrian spokesman replied that there was to be no compromise concerning Tostig.

The king insists, Harold would tell him, that Tostig be restored.

The king must abandon the idea that Tostig will be earl of Northumbria, Harold was told. The king must acknowledge that there is a new earl of Northumbria, Morkere Aelfgarson. Harold was told that he must make that clear to the king. The Northumbrian spokesman would perhaps give the message greater emphasis: the Northumbrians, with their Mercian and Welsh allies, were not asking for Edward's approval of Morkere as earl; they were *demanding* it.

When he was assured that the spokesman spoke for them all, Harold stood to his feet and bade them all goodbye, promising to faithfully relay their words to King Edward.

The rebels were a large force and well equipped, Harold reported to Edward and his counsellors after reciting their demands. He told Edward that the rebels had already moved their forward elements into Oxford and were now thirty-five miles closer to a confrontation with the king.

Edward's response was that he would meet force with force. He perhaps held Harold in his gaze, then shifted to the other Godwinsons, Gyrth and Leofwine, the only earls whose troops, with Harold's, could provide enough strength to counter the combined Northumbrian and Mercian armies. He asked them if they were prepared to fight for the king's right to name his own earls, or would they be intimidated by rebels who had defied the king.

Gyrth and Leofwine would look to Harold to give a response. Doubtlessly with anguish and perhaps with Tostig in the room to hear him, Harold would tell the king that despite his feelings for Tostig as his brother and as a fellow peer, he believed the men of Northumbria had valid grievances and a just cause. He told King Edward that he, Harold, could not in good conscience commit the lives of his men merely to save his brother's position.

Edward perhaps wanted to make sure he was hearing correctly. Did Harold mean that he would not fight?

Yes, Harold would make clear, that was what he was saying; he would not fight this time. Gyrth and Leofwine then let the king know that their feelings were the same as Harold's. They would not fight either.

At that, Tostig's rage likely erupted. He would denounce his brothers, re-accuse Harold of masterminding the entire set of events and charge him with treason.

When calm had been restored, probably after he had ended the meeting and dismissed his counsellors, Edward gave Harold a new mission.

On 28 October 1065 Harold met with Morkere and Edwin and the Northumbrian thanes in Oxford to deliver King Edward's words of capitulation. The rebels' demands had been met. Morkere was confirmed as earl of Northumbria. The king recognised the repeal of the laws instituted by Tostig and the reinstatement of the laws of King Canute in Northumbria. He also granted amnesty to the thanes of Northumbria who had participated in the rebellion.

The rebels got everything they wanted.

Tostig's flight took him first to the royal palace at Westminster, where Judith and the children anxiously waited. He gathered them up, said goodbye to Queen Edith and sailed for Flanders. There, he was sure, Judith's brother, Count Baldwin, would give him asylum for as long as he needed it – which, he vowed, would be only until he could regroup and force his way back into Northumbria.

6
THE CROWNED HEAD
NOVEMBER 1065–JANUARY 1066

Harold had gone to Bosham Manor following All Saints' Day, after Tostig had sailed for Flanders. Perhaps he had tried to see Tostig at Westminster when he returned from Oxford. If so, he had missed him, for Tostig had already collected his family and retainers and left.

Harold doubtless was uneasy about the estrangement from his brother and he was bothered, too, by King Edward's poor health, which had become so obvious that anyone who saw him must have wondered how much longer he could last.

It was perhaps now that Harold began to give increasingly serious thought to the possibility that he might succeed Edward. He would have guessed, if he had not been told, that others were thinking similar thoughts of succession. Besides Duke William and King Harald Hardrada of Norway, there were undoubtedly English aspirants to the crown. Harold had reason to believe that Tostig was one of them. Tostig may well have been thinking that his friendship with Edward and the influence of Queen Edith would in the end win him Edward's endorsement as successor. Harold had witnessed his father perform as a kingmaker and he perhaps at first thought he, too, was limited to that role. But the prospect of Duke William's manipulating his way to the throne unquestionably helped Harold determine that there was no good reason that he, Harold, should not be king. If he talked to Edith Swan's Neck or his close advisers about it, they doubtless encouraged him, pointing out that Edward had no heir and there was no one else with a valid hereditary claim and, in the absence of an heir, Harold was not only the ablest and most deserving possible successor but the most logical one as well. Actually, in many ways he was king already. He was England's chief general and therefore its chief protector, and, Edward excepted, he was the nation's foremost political leader.

It was not merely because William was a Norman that he was the wrong man, Harold's supporters would say. It was because William had never done anything for England, nor had he ever been anything in England. Harold, on the other hand, had served the nation long and well.

Harold often used his manor in Bosham as a meeting place. He met there with Wessex thanes and churchmen, family friends, his overseers and associates of various kinds – merchants, tradesmen, bankers, ship captains – gathering at his invitation or summons. Bosham was also the place to which he called his extended family for social and business affairs. The Godwinson brothers held many interests in common and, except for Tostig from time to time, they usually acted in concert, having discussed the matters and reached a collective decision beforehand. They generally operated on the principle that what was good for one Godwinson was good for them all. Gyrth and Leofwine apparently accepted Harold's seniority willingly. He was the elder brother and was the one responsible for their having received their earldoms, reason enough to defer to him. They evidently trusted his judgement, too. So around the end of November 1065 when Harold likely sent for them, they came to Bosham Manor willingly and expectantly – Gyrth, earl of East Anglia, and Leofwine, earl in Sussex and Kent.

When it was time to get down to business, they agreed that William should not become king and that Harold should. The question was, what must Harold do to become king?

The answer was perhaps obvious. He needed to secure the support of the country's two other major earls – Edwin of Mercia and Morkere of Northumbria, who had already demonstrated their political clout by ousting Tostig and forcing the king to endorse their acts. Edwin and Morkere must be persuaded to go along with the Godwinsons. Furthermore, Harold's cause would be significantly helped if King

Edward were to designate Harold as his successor. The witan could be deeply influenced by that act.

The critical question was: what would Edwin and Morkere require in exchange for their support? That question would have naturally led to another: what did Harold and his brothers have, or what *would* they have if Harold were king, that Edwin and Morkere wanted? The Godwinson brothers would have to think about that for a while.

King Edward usually celebrated Christmas at Gloucester. The hunting was good near there, in the Forest of Dean, and his habit was to spend as much time hunting as he did celebrating. But in December 1065 Edward didn't feel up to either the trip to Gloucester or the hunting. So it was decided that the official celebrations would be held at Westminster instead. And while the king's guests were in town for the Christmas celebrations, his aides decided, the consecration ceremony for the new abbey church at Westminster, the construction of which had been Edward's favourite building project during the past ten years, would be held. The building, on Thorney Island, near the Westminster palace, was at last close enough to completion to be consecrated and used. Some had feared that Edward would not live long enough to see the structure finished or to witness its great nave filled with worshipers and the presence of the Almighty, which was Edward's dream, but now, praise God, Edward would behold that spectacle after all, or so it was thought.

The guest list for the celebration and the dedication was long. It included most of the brightest luminaries, both lay and clerical, of English society: the archbishop of Canterbury; the archbishop of York; eight bishops; eight abbots; five earls; distinguished thanes; leading citizens and landholders; and assorted government officials. Among them were representatives of the country's sundry ethnic, professional and business interests, a wide cross-section of the nation's influentials.

The occasion would not be just a holy one, or even a completely festive one. For the nation's influentials the event would provide a time to exchange information, make contacts and arrange deals. Harold and his brothers, the two earls, were going. So were Morkere and Edwin. Harold planned to see them there, confident that he and they could come to an agreement about Edward's successor.

Christmas of 1065 fell on a Sunday. Harold had arranged to meet with Edwin and Morkere on Boxing Day, which was Monday, while

Edward would be occupied with distributing Christmas gifts to members of his staff. On Christmas Eve, however, Edward fell suddenly and seriously ill. When Harold saw him, needing help to move and barely able to speak intelligibly, he asked Edwin and Morkere to meet with him and Gyrth and Leofwine that evening.

They quickly got down to business. Edwin and Morkere, learning of Edward's condition, realised the urgency of the situation. Harold would certainly have pointed out to them that there was no time to waste. They could not afford to wait even one hour longer to decide who would be king after Edward, so obviously imminent was his death. Harold put his plan before them, saying that if the five of them – three Godwinson brothers and two Aelfgarson brothers – could agree, the witan would go along with them. Harold then asked Edwin and Morkere to support him.

Edwin and Morkere apparently had not come to the meeting either unsuspecting or unprepared. In response to Harold's solicitation of their support, they made a request. As part of an agreement between them and Harold and his brothers, they wanted assurance that their father's grandson, the great-grandson of their grandfather, Earl Leofric, would become king after Harold.

Edwin or Morkere would explain. Their sister, Lady Alditha, widow of King Griffith ap Llewellyn, was without a husband. Edwin and Morkere wanted Harold to take her as his wife and queen. She would bear him a son, and that son would become king after Harold. That was the deal the Aelfgarsons put up to Harold.

Edith Swan's Neck and Harold had known each other since they were children. Her father had been one of Earl Godwin's thanes and a regular guest at Bosham Manor. When she and Harold were teenagers, Harold evidently became more than a friend. If he had other girls, or women later, which Edith might have sometimes suspected, she was comforted by the knowledge that she was the only constant one, the one he always came back to, the one he confided in, depended on and treated with respect. She was the one who had given him children. She was the one who was mistress of his manor. But the two of them had never been married, or at least they had never gone through a wedding ceremony.

His reason for not having a traditional marriage she perhaps never knew. It might have been that he didn't think a ceremony or the

Church's sanction was important. Perhaps he considered her his wife and himself her husband and a church wedding to him was simply unnecessary. Later on, he may have felt it would be awkward to have a wedding after years of living together and having had children together. For her part, Edith may have felt that if he was happy with the way they lived, it was good enough for her. Having him was what evidently mattered most.

Duke William had already made it clear to Harold that his arrangement with Edith Swan's Neck was no bar to a Church-sanctioned marriage. He was free, in effect, to remarry.

If Edith Swan's Neck was allowed to express an opinion on the matter, she may well have urged Harold to accept the Aelfgarsons' proposal. Harold's decision would affect not only her and him. It would affect the entire country. Edith would have realised the ramifications and might have pointed them out to Harold. In addition to what his accession to the throne would mean for England, it would also accomplish what Harold's father had tried to do when he talked Edward into marrying Harold's sister: it would give the crown to the house of Godwin, beginning with Harold and continuing through a son of his. Without a doubt, it was what Godwin would have advised his son to do.

It was, Edith likely agreed, something Harold had to do.

With Edward on his last legs, Harold and his brothers were trapped in a poor bargaining position. As soon as Edward was in his grave, which could be any day, they would have the Bastard to contend with, whether Harold was king or not. Taking on a resistant Northumbria and Mercia and the duke of Normandy all at the same time would be a task too formidable to contemplate. Without the resources of the Crown – which included the Royal Navy, the Royal Treasury and the authority to order out the fyrd – Harold likely considered the task little short of suicidal.

Edwin and Morkere knew that Harold had his back against the wall and they knew that Harold knew it.

By Christmas afternoon Edward had improved enough to attend the Christmas service in the new abbey church and the banquet that evening, and Harold began to hope that the crisis could be staved off for a while, giving him more time to manoeuvre with the witan, even perhaps time to have Edward designate him as successor.

However the next day, Boxing Day, Edward's condition worsened, and he had to be carried to his chambers before the gift distribution was completed.

Wednesday of that week was 28 December, Holy Innocents' Day, the day on which the Church commemorated the deaths of the children slain by King Herod after the wise men from the East had enquired about the birth of the Christ child. It was also the day that King Edward's staff had scheduled the consecration of the new Church of St Peter the Apostle, as Edward called the magnificent new abbey church, though it would come to be popularly known simply as Westminster Abbey.

King Edward was far too ill to attend the service. He was slipping in and out of consciousness, and it was anyone's guess among his physicians and counsellors at what hour his soul would escape his infirm body.

Harold, seeing Edward, though clinging to life, seeming already a corpse, decided he could wait no longer, not even till the consecration was out of the way. He summoned the Aelfgarson brothers before the service and announced to them that he was accepting their offer of support and he was promising to show them his gratitude and to earn theirs as well.

At the conclusion of the consecration service, in response to a summons, Harold hurried to the palace and found Edward lying in his bed. In the room with the king, standing or sitting, were several clergymen, including the archbishop of Canterbury and a number of court officials and vassals, and Queen Edith.

The archbishop, Stigand, a man indebted to Harold's father for the advancement of his clerical career, told Harold that the king was delirious, that he had been telling them about a wild dream he had had.

The king's eyes opened then and while everyone in the room watched, his lips parted and he grasped Queen Edith's hand. 'May God reward my wife for her loving service to me,' he managed to get out. 'She's been a devoted daughter to me.'

Edward withdrew his hand from Edith's and reached out for Harold's. Harold stepped closer and let the king weakly take it.

'My faithful Harold,' he said in a feeble voice, 'I'm turning over to you the responsibility for the queen. And the whole kingdom. I'm placing them under your protection.' His eyes rolled toward the others in the room, then came back to Harold. 'Take care of these men. They served me well. Many of them came from Normandy to be with me. Let them serve you the same way they served me if they want to.' It was evidently an effort to get the words out. 'If they don't want to stay,' Edward said, 'let them go back to Normandy with their property. Will you do that for me?'

Harold answered simply, 'I will.'

At that, the king's lips formed a momentary smile and his eyes closed. While Harold stood watching the dying king, Archbishop Stigand slipped to Harold's side and whispered into his ear, 'You need to assemble the witan. Quickly. I'll announce to them that the king has designated you as his successor. The queen and these men are your witnesses.'

A national witanagemot, attended by those in town for the Christmas celebrations, was held the next day, and the archbishop of Canterbury told the group that King Edward had made his wishes known and done so in the company of witnesses. Of his own free will the king had commended into Earl Harold's keeping the nation and its people.

Earl Edwin would also have spoken to the witan. He would have told them that the men of Mercia desired to honour the wishes of the king and support the selection of Earl Harold to be king following their beloved Edward. The men of Northumbria, Earl Morkere would have said, joined their Mercian neighbours in urging the selection of Earl Harold to be king.

The witan voted and reached a decision. Harold Godwinson, earl of Wessex, was their overwhelming choice.

Sometime during the dark early morning hours of Thursday 5 January 1066, on the eve of Epiphany, Edward's beloved God called him home.

The funeral was held on Friday morning, 6 January, the day of Epiphany. The lifeless body, tightly wrapped in a shroud, was carried head first on an open bier borne by eight pallbearers, the bier lavishly decorated with embroidered palls and surmounted with two silver crosses, one above the head of the corpse, one above the feet. Two acolytes, each with a pair of knelling bells, followed the bier. Behind them in solemn procession walked a group of tonsured clerics led by the abbot of the Westminster abbey, and behind them, dirge-singing choristers, all slowly proceeding from the Westminster palace to the new Church of St Peter the Apostle.

Inside, following the singing of the funeral mass, as the crowd of mourners looked on, King Edward's body, redolent with aromatic oils and ointments, was laid to rest in a stone sarcophagus, a sceptre at his right side and a crown on his head, symbols of his vacated office, and lowered into the tomb reserved for it beneath the floor in front of the main altar. His death had come so swiftly following the church's completion there was no inscription on the slab that covered the tomb.

Nearly a hundred years later, on 7 February 1161, after a long campaign conducted by generations of his admirers, who thought of him as a good and holy man, Edward would be canonised by Pope Alexander III. He would become, for all time, St Edward the Confessor. His mortal remains lie in his Church of St Peter the Apostle – Westminster Abbey – to this day.

Now England would have a new king.

Archbishop Stigand told Harold that the coronation should be held as soon as possible. Harold could not be officially crowned until the late king was laid to rest. But once that was done, the archbishop urged, the coronation should immediately follow. An old king's funeral and a new king's coronation would be held the same day.

The site would be the new abbey church. It was convenient. It would provide a proper setting. It was Edward's place of repose. Having the coronation there would suggest continuity from Edward to Harold. It was fitting. It might even set a precedent, which of course it did.

The throng that only hours before had streamed out of the new church at the conclusion of Edward's funeral now streamed back in. A centuries-old ritual, rooted in the Old Testament no less than in secular tradition, was about to begin.

The two archbishops, Stigand of Canterbury and Eldred of York, led Harold into the church, down the centre aisle, at the head of the procession. Harold wore a red and green robe around his shoulders, fastened with a jewelled rectangular clasp below his throat. Behind him trailed a company of clerics and behind them the choir, singing an anthem from the Psalms as they proceeded, beseeching the Almighty to grant the new king strength, justice, mercy and wisdom.

At the foot of the main altar, standing near the spot where the late king lay beneath the slabs of stone, the archbishops and Harold prostrated themselves before the altar while the other clergy and the choir proceeded around and past them.

Now Archbishop Eldred rose and mounted the high altar as the words of the *Te Deum* rose from the choir loft: 'We praise Thee, O God. Thee, O God, we acknowledge...'

Harold, with Archbishop Stigand beside him, then rose. Harold turned to face the congregation, and Archbishop Eldred in a booming voice asked the people if they accepted Harold as their king, to rule over them.

'We do!' The crowd shouted in unrehearsed response. 'We do!'

Harold turned again and mounted the altar to stand beside Eldred. He placed his hand upon a treasured copy of the Gospels and read aloud his vows as king. He promised to prohibit under the law the wrongdoing of all people within his dominion. He promised to apply the laws even-handedly, without favouritism, without regard for rank or class. He promised to leaven his justice with mercy, in the same way that he would ask Almighty God to render mercy unto him.

At the end of his oaths, the people shouted, 'Amen!'

Then Harold knelt, and the bishops began their individual prayers. They asked for God's guidance for the new king. They asked for peace in his time. They asked for the preservation of his health and for his long life and for the bolstering of his spiritual welfare. They asked that the new king would defend the nation against all enemies. They asked that he would defend the Church against its enemies. They asked that God empower and equip him for every necessary task. They asked for God's blessing on the king and the country. When at last they were done, Archbishop Eldred recited a prayer that went something like this:

O God, our rock and our salvation, by whose power we live and move and have our being, in whose ways we delight and in whose will we daily strive to be, Eternal Father, Lord and Creator, Sustainer and Deliverer, we do now in all earnestness humbly pray that you will grant unto your servant Harold your holy favour and bless him our king with every grace and strength to reign over us in justice and in peace with both man and God. Ordain him, maintain him and make him our king, mighty and strong, just and good, merciful and beneficent. In the name of Christ our Lord, amen.

The choir began singing an anthem drawn from the accounts of the anointing of King Solomon by Zadok the priest and Nathan the prophet, in First Kings 1 and First Chronicles 29. While they sang, Archbishop Eldred stepped toward Harold holding a cruse of holy oil and, as Harold remained on his knees, he poured the chrism onto Harold's bowed head.

The archbishop offered another prayer and Harold was helped to his feet. The bishops brought forward the royal vestments, the coronation robe, coat and stole, and one by one placed them on him. Then the regalia were brought to him – the ring, the sword, the crown, the sceptre and the rod, emblems of his exalted office. The ring was placed upon his finger and the sword fastened to his gold-buckled belt. Then Archbishop Eldred took the crown in both hands and raised it above his head to display it to the entire congregation. He prayed again, then firmly placed the crown upon Harold's head.

The choir burst into another anthem, this one inspired by the words in First Kings 1, and Daniel 3, verse 9: 'May the king live forever!'

As the whole assembly stood, King Harold stepped down from the altar and, led by the noblemen who had supported him, men of the witan and others, he proceeded – the sceptre in one hand, the royal orb in the other, the crown upon his head, the royal sword at his waist, the royal robe on his shoulders – back to the palace and inside it to the throne on the dais in the great hall.

In the procession's wake a throng of subjects of the new king eagerly followed, excitedly swept along by the magnificent event. Some would find their way into the palace for the banquet; many others would participate in the celebration's overflow on the palace grounds.

One witness to the coronation spurned the celebration. He flung himself upon a horse and sped off to find a ship stout enough and a crew brave enough to bear him across the stormy Channel to the shore of Normandy.

7

THE OVERSEAS REACTION
JANUARY 1066

Duke William had heard from Harold only once since Harold had returned to England more than a year earlier. William had sent him a message asking about his progress in establishing a Norman garrison at Dover, as Harold had promised to do. Harold had sent back an evasive answer. Since then, there had been no word from him, and William apparently had no idea of what Harold was up to.

On Monday 9 January 1066, William was at his estate at Quevilly, outside Rouen, when one of his staff members came to him and told him that someone had just arrived from London with news. To William it came as good news that King Edward had at last departed this life and had thereby vacated the throne. The bad news was that Harold had immediately filled the vacancy.

According to one account, William had been ready to leave on a hunt with a large group of his associates when the news reached him. The surprise in his face quickly turned to anger. He unthinkingly fastened his cloak, then as if changing his mind, he unfastened it again. Without saying a word to the others in his hunting party, who themselves were silent, apparently afraid to speak, he stormed off, took a boat to the other side of the River Seine and entered his palace. He sat down on a bench and stretched his cloak across his face, furious and stunned, scalding thoughts bubbling in his head.

Once the rage subsided to a level where reason could return to his angry thoughts, William summoned his closest confidants and advisors to help him decide a course of action. By the time they arrived, they would have already had a chance to think about the situation. Odo, the duke's half-brother who was the bishop of Bayeux, and Robert of Mortain, the other half-brother, would have been there; so too would William fitz Osbern and Robert, count of Eu, probably the most senior man at the meeting and the most experienced soldier. Robert probably provided an evaluation of their chances of overthrowing King Harold. He would realise that it would take a substantial force to have any chance of beating Harold on his own ground. He would remind the duke that the Saxons, as he called them, were no pushovers. Not only were they first-class soldiers, but there were a lot more of them than there were of Normans. Also, he would point out, the Saxons' supply lines would be much shorter than the Normans' and not subject to interdiction or loss at sea.

Someone might have asked if the people of England, the nobles and the fighting men, supported Harold and would fight for him, or did Harold's coronation mean only that he had managed a successful palace coup.

A knowing member of the group could have given an accurate answer. The men of Wessex, the people of Harold's own earldom, were bound to be with him entirely. His brothers, Earl Gyrth and Earl Leofwine, would bring their armies to his side. The two minor earls, Waltheof and Oswulf, were insignificant. Their holdings were too small, their resources too meagre. They didn't matter. The question marks were Earl Edwin of Mercia and Earl Morkere of Northumbria. They did matter, and it was anybody's guess what they would do in a showdown.

If William acted characteristically, he would at sometime during the discussion have let his advisors know his feelings. He probably told them that he wanted to learn what the problems were, that he wanted to know what they were up against. But in clear and emphatic words he declared that they were going to go to England no matter what. He is likely to have told them that they were not going only if the odds were right or only if it looked like a sure thing – they were going regardless. Win or lose, they were going after the duplicitous Harold.

The only question to be decided was how best to go after him. Count Robert of Eu perhaps offered some advice. Three things were needed, he would say: first an army, one that was much stronger than that which William had at the moment; second a navy, one large enough to transport an entire army and its supplies across the Channel all at once; and third, a miracle of God.

It would take a miracle, or something very close to one, to get a fleet of the necessary size, carrying an army of the necessary size – including men, horses, supplies and equipment – safely to the other side of the Channel, to the spot where they intended to land, intact, with men, animals and equipment immediately ready for battle. It would be a tall order indeed.

If it was a miracle that was required, William might well have responded, then they would pray for that miracle. Those who couldn't pray would have to learn.

More practically, William issued basic orders to the group, doubtlessly assigning tasks to each man present. He told them he wanted an army – cavalry, infantry, bowmen – powerful enough to crush whatever awaited him across the Channel. If such an army couldn't be raised among the men of Normandy, they were to hire mercenaries. They were to recruit every soldier of fortune, every Viking-hearted rowdy to be found from the shores of Normandy all the way to the Mediterranean Sea. They were to enlist every younger son who was wondering what there would be for him when his father died and his oldest brother inherited the estate. The recruiters were to promise land, property, title – all the spoils of which they could think. What he wanted, the duke made clear, was every land-hungry, money-hungry, power-hungry, fighting man who could sit on a horse or march behind one. He wanted every restless, roving-eyed adventurer, every drifter, every ne'er-do-well, every malcontent steady enough to wield a sword or stretch a bow. Whoever they were, wherever they were, he wanted them.

He gave orders to assemble a naval fleet big enough to deliver that army to Harold's doorstep. They were to borrow, buy or build it. Whatever it took.

There was something else William emphasised: there was no time to lose. They had to be in England before autumn and bad weather arrived. They *had* to be.

If the duke didn't mention it, someone else undoubtedly pointed out that they also needed to be aware of the appearance of things. They needed to give some consideration to how this invasion of England would look to other people – to the French, for example, to the Germans and Spaniards and Italians. And to the Pope. They would have to be careful that they were not seen as aggressors, as usurpers, lest their actions cost them the sympathy and support, however tacit, of important others. In very practical terms, they did not want someone on their flank or behind them suddenly sympathising with Harold.

William had probably already thought of that. If so, he assured the group that they would proceed carefully. They should tell people what they were doing and why. They should tell people, their own and others, everything they needed to know. They should tell it so that everyone would understand why they were doing what they were doing. Everyone must know that they were going to England because there was no alternative; Harold had left them no alternative.

They would even tell Harold. William was going to give him a chance to back down. It was perhaps at that point that Duke William summoned William Malet into the meeting. Malet was lord of Graville-Sainte-Honorine, near Le Havre. He would take on a delicate mission for the duke.

Malet had family connections in England. He knew the country; he'd been there many times. He knew the language. He also knew Harold. As William's envoy, Malet was to get an audience with Harold and tell him that Duke William understood his wanting to take over for King Edward, to relieve the poor man's suffering mind as he lay dying. It had been an act of kindness to King Edward. However, now that King Edward had passed on, it was time for Harold to honour those promises that he had made to the duke, promises made on holy relics, sworn before God. They were binding, irrevocable, sacred promises – promises which, if violated, carried grave consequences. Malet, under Duke William's instructions, would remind Harold of those oaths and of their seriousness.

William had no reason to think that Harold would bow out. The Malet mission was a public relations ploy. No one, including the Pope, would be able to say Duke William hadn't tried to settle the matter without resort to arms and bloodshed. The duke had apparently thought of everything.

8

THE CHANNEL
PREHISTORY TO 1066

Long before the story of man in the British Isles began, there was the land, which over the span of eons had alternated between periods of glaciation and verdure. There was also the sea, which unrelentingly washed and pounded the edges of the land, shaping and reshaping it. The land always was, since Creation. But there was not always the sea, at least not a sea that surrounded and isolated the land.

More than a million years before humans first arrived in that land, there existed a vast plain that stretched from the coasts of France, Belgium and the Netherlands to the shores of south-eastern England, making of the island of today a northward projecting peninsula joined to the Continent, like a thumb to a hand, at Europe's north-western edge. Through that low and lush plain streamed the Rhine from the south and the Thames from the west, meeting and mingling on the plain to form one river flowing north.

Across that plain, Palaeolithic clans – carrying the flint tools and weapons that marked theirs as the early Stone Age – wandered from Europe proper in pursuit of game with which to feed themselves and shield their bodies from the wet and the cold. Those Palaeolithic men and women were the first humans on the land that for hundreds of millennia had stood ripe for discovery, awaiting man's coming.

After the early Stone Age people, perhaps 10,000 years before Christ, came their technological successors, Mesolithic and Neolithic men and women, who created the wheel, discovered how to make pottery, invented and learned to use bows and arrows, learned to domesticate animals and to cultivate fruit-bearing trees and grain-bearing plants and learned how to spin and weave and make cloth. They were the middle and late Stone Age people, and it was following their arrival in the land that the great cataclysm occurred.

At the time, the Atlantic Ocean reached into the continental landmass to form a gulf at what is now the western end of the English Channel. Long and eastward probing, the gulf thrust deep into the side of north-western Europe, with south-western England on its north shore, Brittany and Normandy on its south shore, and the coastlines of both shores continually changing in shape and distance, altered by the sea's pressing tides and the earth's subsurface tumults. At the eastern limits of the gulf the sea washed against an enormous chalky ridge, beyond which lay the low plain that connected that thumblike peninsula to the Continent.

Then the plain began to sink. The gradual but massive subsidence allowed the waters of the North Sea, itself a gulf of the Atlantic, bounding the peninsula on the east, like the space between thumb and index finger, to creep southward, deepening and spreading till at last it flooded the plain, leaving the chalk ridge, running north-west to south-east, from Kent to Picardy, as the last link from the peninsula to the Continent.

Irresistibly the east-seeking gulf tides and storm-driven gulf seas assaulted the ridge until it was finally breached. Once the first crack occurred, the gulf waters rushed through to meet the surge of the North Sea on the other side of the ridge. A powerful tide race was thus created, which, with each ebb and flood, sent the sea tearing wildly through the gap, ripping away huge chunks of the chalk ridge, widening the separation until the gulf and the North Sea were one and the parts of the land were two, one the European mainland, the other an island, and the gulf became the English Channel (or La Manche, the Sleeve, as the French called it).

Ever restless, the Channel kept changing, and does so still, eating into the land and widening itself, particularly upchannel, toward the east, where soils of chalk, sandstone and clay are relatively soft and therefore more vulnerable to erosion by rainfall as well as the pounding sea. At the western end of the Channel, the oldest part, shorelines are rockier, their granite edges standing more firmly against the washing and battering of the sea.

The shores on both sides of the Channel vary, from enormous and forbidding rock formations, to more hospitable shingle or sand beaches, to low or towering cliffs, all interrupted at odd intervals by estuaries. Of the two shorelines, the English is the straighter and the French shore the more irregular, with jutting capes and deeply curved bays.

From the rocky islet of Ushant, off the coast of Brittany, and Land's End, at the western-most tip of England, the Channel stretches some 350 miles to the North Sea. At its western entrance the Channel is ninety miles wide and elsewhere ranges from one hundred miles at its widest point to twenty-one miles at its narrowest, which is the Strait of Dover, where the 700-800-foot-high chalk cliffs on the English shore mark the sea's breach of the chalky ridge and which, on a clear day, can be seen with the naked eye from the other end of the breach on the French side of the Channel.

Once the land had become an island, or a set of islands, newcomers to it had to cross miles of sea to reach it. Ironically, however, the Channel proved to be an avenue for invasion rather than a barrier to it.

The first to cross were the Celts. In massive numbers, perhaps beginning around 1,000 BC, from their home in south-west Germany, they swept over northern and central Europe and gave Europe its first civilisation north of the Alps (which is the Celtic word for 'mountains'). South of the Alps, of course, there were the other civilisations of Europe, including those of Greece and Rome. To the Greeks the Celts were Keltoi, or barbarians; to the Romans they were Galli, or Gauls. They were, according to Roman writers of their time, a race of tall, fair-haired warriors, strong, fierce and savage, who sped to battle in chariots and often fought naked, and who were renowned for their metal-working ability, first in bronze and later in iron, and for their inventiveness and art as well as for their prowess in combat.

They comprised an assortment of tribes united by their language, by common customs and traditions and by a fanatical, bloody pagan religion presided over by a class of priests, the Druids. The tribes were many, but they fell within two major language groups, Gaels and

Britons, each group speaking its own version of the same Celtic language, either Gaelic or Brythonic.

The early Celtic invaders fashioned crude seagoing craft, their hulls covered by hides and sealed with animal fat to make them watertight, and paddled them across the Channel, and eventually Celts spread over the whole of the British Isles, the Britons among them giving the islands their name and occupying present England and Wales, the Gaels settling in Ireland and Scotland.

The Romans were next to cross. In 55 BC, Gaius Julius Caesar was then proconsul, or military governor, of Gaul, the western European Celtic stronghold that Caesar and his legions had won from the Celts in genocidal warfare and had forced to become a Roman province. He turned a wondering and adventurous eye toward a land about which he had heard marvellous reports but which he had never seen – the land that Romans called Britannia and Celts called Albion. It was the island home of the Britons, fierce warriors who dyed their bodies blue with woad before hurling themselves into combat. It was a land of magnificent forests, verdant fields, rich minerals, even gold, agricultural abundance and agreeable weather. Caesar decided he had to see it for himself.

In late August 55 BC, standing on the shore of the Strait of Dover, his way clear, the towering white cliffs of the storied island in view in the distance, Caesar launched his expeditionary force, an army of two Roman legions, about 10,000 men, including cavalry and infantry, aboard eighty transport vessels. As the Roman ships drew into shore, a force of Britons rushed into the surf in their chariots to repel them.

A furious struggle ensued, with the Romans forcing the defenders back onto the beach in disarray, compelling the Britons to yield and ask for terms. During the crucial hours of negotiation, while commanders of the two sides talked, Caesar and his legionaries discovered that the blue-skinned Britons were not the only adversary they faced. The Channel itself had risen against them.

Huge tides caused by a full moon, characteristic of the Channel, caught Caesar and his captains unawares and unprepared. Many of their ships lying at anchor off the beach were seized by the monstrous tide and had their anchor cables snapped, their anchors ripped from them and were dashed against one another or onto the shore and shattered. At the sight of their ships' destruction, the legionaries, struck by the sudden realisation that they might now be stranded, were swept by dismay.

The Britons quickly seized the advantage. They strode out of the negotiating session and led their fighters back into combat against the dispirited Romans. Caesar and his officers, however, exerting the legendary discipline of Rome's legions, were able to rally their troops and again force the Britons to submit after days of fighting.

A year later Caesar returned to Britain with new resolve and a stronger force, this time with an army of *five* legions, about 25,000 men, cavalry and infantry, aboard a fleet of 800 ships. The legions landed on the Kentish shore unopposed, but, as in the year earlier, soon fell under assault by the sea. A storm engulfed Caesar's fleet, which lay at anchor offshore, destroying or damaging a large part of it, and Caesar, who had penetrated some twelve miles inland with his troops, was obliged to return to the landing site to salvage as much of the fleet as he could. After securing the fleet, Caesar resumed his march into Britain's hinterland. His army ran into opposition from a British force marshalled by the Celtic chieftain Cassivellaunus, which repeatedly struck the Roman columns with hit-and-run chariot attacks but could not stop the Roman advance. When Cassivellaunus at last realised he couldn't withstand Caesar's army, he struck a deal, submitting to Caesar. Satisfied that he had conquered Britain, Caesar ordered his men, their horses and their equipment back onto their ships and recrossed the Channel without incident.

Nearly a hundred years passed before the Romans returned to Britain, but when they did, in AD 43, they set out on a campaign of subjugation and occupation. By AD 84 they had conquered all of present England and part of Scotland and had made Britain a province of Rome and were systematically imposing Roman civilisation upon it.

The new occupiers of the land now had to face the same menace as those before them: invasion from the sea. This time it was Angles, Saxons and Jutes, Germanic peoples from Schleswig, Holstein and Jutland, who would in later times be lumped together in a common identifying term – Anglo-Saxons. The new invaders at first raided, then settled and were there to stay. By 410, when Rome withdrew its forces to defend itself on the Continent, the time of the Romans in Britain was over.

What followed then was 400 years of steady Anglo-Saxon ascendancy, while the land's Celtic population, Romanised and otherwise, was absorbed, killed or pushed to the western extremities of the island, particularly Wales, but also Cornwall and Devon. To the part of the island that the Anglo-Saxons dominated, the vast part, they gave a new name, Angleland, or England, and a new language, English.

In the eighth century the dominance of the Anglo-Saxons was for the first time successfully challenged. This time the invaders were the Vikings. From Norway, Sweden and Denmark they came, master seamen, master warriors, striking out across the North Sea, into the Atlantic and into the Channel, assaulting the coasts of England, Scotland and Ireland, coming first, as had the Anglo-Saxons, to pillage, eventually to settle.

In the year 1066 the English Channel and the North Sea, history's broad avenues of assault on the British Isles, remained temptingly open to any new invader who dared seek to usurp the land again. The historic dangers in attempting conquest also remained, on the sea and on the land.

If Duke William were to go to England as an invader while King Harold reigned, he would have to go as Caesar had gone, and face obstacles in all ways similar to those Caesar had faced. Caesar had gone not as part of a migrating horde, as had all the others, predecessor and successor alike, but as an intended conqueror, purposing to be master of all, the land and the people. Like the Romans who had followed Caesar a hundred years after his time, William would be going not to supplant the island's people but to rule them.

To do so, he would have to go with a huge, diverse force of fighting men, infantry, cavalry, bowmen and engineers: an army that could meet Harold's superior numbers with what William believed to be superior Norman fighting power, as Caesar had done against the Britons with his outnumbered but highly trained, disciplined legions. William's army would have to go with enough provisions to sustain itself until it had gained enough ground to support itself with forage, as Caesar's army had done. Like Caesar, William could not assume one great decisive battle; he would have to plan for a protracted conflict, a series of battles. He therefore would have to find a defensible base on the shore and quickly secure it from attack, as Caesar had done, lest the invaders be thrust back into the sea whence they had come. The campaign would have to start from that base.

Before any campaign could begin, however, William and his invasion army, like Caesar and his, would have to *get* to England. Getting there meant that everyone and everything that was needed to wage a successful campaign would have to be put aboard ships and the ships put into the sea, which with the weather, as Caesar had learned, could prove the most destructive foe of all.

A chief factor in the launching of an invasion fleet would be the wind. William's ships would be shallow-draft sailing vessels, un-oared, unlike the Romans' ships and those of the Anglo-Saxons and the Vikings. Because of the Norman vessels' shallow draft, they possessed little or no tacking capability and they would require a steady southerly wind to carry the invaders northward across the Channel. The wind must be fair, but not too strong, lest the sea be roiled and the open boats be subject to swamping.

The Channel's tides and currents would be an enormously important factor as well. The strongest tides, those that ran with the greatest force, occurred at the time of the new moon and the full moon, about a fortnight apart, when the moon and sun were in conjunction or in opposition, and at those times the Channel would see its highest and its lowest tides. The range between high and low tides in the Channel could exceed thirty feet. The gentler tides, the neaps, whose flood and ebb would not vary so greatly, occurred during the moon's first- and third-quarter phases. Timing could be crucial in the launching of the invasion fleet and in its landing. Critical also would be the place of its launching. Near some potential launching sites coastal islands created violent tide races that would sweep vessels along in their speeding flow, and certain capes caused deadly crosscurrents as the tide crashed against the land, then, repelled, rushed back on itself, rendering sailing ships, even oared vessels, virtually uncontrollable and casting their crews and cargoes on the mercy of the wild sea.

Squalls and gales could rise suddenly at sea and blow ships miles off course, forcing them far from their intended destination and thus giving knowing seamen reason never to say they were 'going to' whatever their destination but only that they were 'going toward' it. Wise Channel sailors never boasted about what they would do concerning the sea.

Besides the unpredictable storms that could run vessels aground on sandbanks or hurl them against shattering rocks, the Channel was also menaced by blinding, disorienting fog that could swiftly swallow up men and vessels. Veteran Channel sailors knew that in warm-weather months, which was when Duke William intended to cross, they could expect to encounter fog about one day out of every five.

William, ever a realist and possessed with far greater intelligence concerning the Channel than Caesar had had when he stood poised for the invasion of Britain, knew full well that to succeed with his invasion he must regard the Channel not as a friend but as a duplicitous ally, as treacherous as it was useful.

9
THE WAR PLAN
JANUARY 1066–FEBRUARY 1066

The Duchess Matilda had come from a good background. Her father was Baldwin V, count of Flanders, widely considered a man wise in statecraft and the ways of ambitious men. Her mother was the Countess Adela, daughter of Robert I, king of France. Having grown up in an atmosphere of power and politics, Matilda was unawed by the men who dealt in them, though she had great admiration for such men. When she was seventeen years old, her father the count, seeing an opportunity to make a potentially powerful and much-needed new ally, gave her in marriage to William II, duke of Normandy, then twenty-two years old and himself in need of allies. It was a beneficial arrangement for both parties, but it was a purely political marriage. Or so it seemed at first.

Matilda and William were distant cousins, both descendants of the legendary Viking chieftain Rollo, the first duke of Normandy. Aside from that, they appeared to have little in common, she an almost freakishly small young woman, standing four foot two, he a large young man, five foot ten and husky, a physical mismatch; she having been nurtured in a traditional family, he having lived with the stigma of bastardy and having grown up as a virtual orphan fostered by strong men whose fortunes depended on his survival, an emotional mismatch. Yet the marriage had succeeded.

There had never been even a hint of scandal concerning their marriage, his father's eye for the girls apparently not having been passed on to William. And Matilda's unusual proportions hadn't prevented her from mothering a slew of children. She and William had four sons and five daughters. The only stain on the marriage, and it proved temporary, was placed on it by the Church of Rome, which, objecting to a second marriage by Matilda's grandfather, had for years withheld recognition of Matilda's marriage to William. The duke finally got that matter straightened out and, in 1059, no less a person than Pope Nicholas II himself pronounced the Church's blessing on the union.

Those who knew them well knew there was something, some quality, unperceived by even those who knew them best, that bound Matilda and William more closely than was ordinary in marriages between obviously well-matched partners. Of course Matilda and William alone knew what that quality was, the display of it occurring only behind closed doors.

She no doubt was a participant in his counsels, and one may imagine the two of them in William's castle residence at Bonneville-sur-Touques, discussing his plans for deposing King Harold. She might well have sought an answer to a fundamental question: why do you want to do this? She would desperately want to know why he would risk all that he had merely to gain more. Was it pure anger that drove him, or hatred or jealousy or simple vanity or what? Did he even know what it was that was driving him?

He probably did know. He likely knew himself well enough to realise that a lot of things were driving him. One of them was certainly anger. She and everyone else close to him knew that. If he acknowledged the anger, Matilda may well have told him that anger was not a good enough reason to risk his life and everything else that he had, including his friends. He was confident that he was angry with good reason. Harold had betrayed him, lied to him and double-crossed him. He'd be damned if Harold was going to get away with all that.

She might have called that vanity. He wouldn't see it as vanity. It was making Harold pay for trying to take what was rightfully his. It was showing Harold, and anyone else who might be tempted, that Duke William couldn't be double-crossed, out-manoeuvred or bested in any way. If that was vanity, then he was willing to be put down as the bastard who was driven by vanity.

With additional thought, however, he is likely to have conceded other feelings. He had lived with them long enough. He is very likely to have admitted that part of his driving force was his wanting more than what his father had given him. He would accept what was his by virtue of being his father's son, of course. He had that coming to him. But he obviously wanted something that wasn't his father's, or *his* father's before him. He wanted something of his own. He knew what his father had been and he was certain that he was, despite the handicap of bastardy, a better man than his father. Becoming king would prove it. By God then, a king was what he was going to be. He was determined.

Having been won over, or having accepted the futility of trying to dissuade him, Matilda would ask what she could do to help. He told her that he wanted her to keep fourteen-year-old Robert, their eldest son, safe. If something did happen to William, Robert was to succeed him as duke of Normandy. He would leave behind some good men (Roger of Beaumont, Roger of Montgomery and Hugh of Avranches) to help Matilda in his absence and to help Robert. He had already required Normandy's leading barons to pledge their support of Robert. It was important for William to know that Robert was protected and would become duke after him.

Matilda wanted to do something more tangible. If William couldn't think of what that might be, she herself would come up with something. She would give him a special ship that she would pay for herself. It would be his flagship. What's more, she would name it. It would be called *Mora*. (The meaning of 'mora' remains uncertain. Some speculation has it that it was a term of mild opprobrium, perhaps something Matilda had been called as a misbehaving child.)

If she asked what else he needed, William probably would have told her what his cousin, the count of Eu, had told him. He would need, besides an army and a navy, a miracle. Matilda then, perhaps, was the one who told him to go and ask the Pope, as God's head man, to give him one. William may have replied, with honesty, that he was doing what he could to keep the Pope *out* of his business and that the last thing he wanted was to involve the Pope. He would explain that the Pope took a dim view of Christians fighting Christians and that the Pope was very liable to blame William and order sanctions against him if he took an army to England to do exactly that of which the Pope took a dim view. William would tell Matilda that he did not want the Pope interfering.

Matilda is likely to have called that attitude nonsense. What William didn't want was the Pope interfering on behalf of someone else. What he *did* want was the Pope to interfere on *his* behalf. So he should do what he could to get the Pope on his side.

The abbey at Le Bec-Hellouin, on the River Risle, about twenty miles south-west of Rouen, had begun in the heart of the Norman knight Herluin, who in 1034, heeding a divine call, had abandoned his old life and given himself to the service of God. By 1060 the Christian community that Herluin founded had become the most famous monastery in western Europe. One of the big reasons for its being so and for its being sought after by clerical aspirants from all over Europe, was the presence there of the brilliant Italian scholar, theologian and teacher who became the abbey's prior, under Herluin. He was Lanfranc, an impressive man regarded by those who knew him, or knew of him, as a saintly genius, a man of eloquence, uncommon good sense, sound judgement, profound insight, immense knowledge and pure motive. Among the important people who knew him was Duke William, who knew him well.

William had become familiar with the Le Bec abbey while he was directing the siege of Brionne, four miles upriver from Le Bec-Hellouin. This campaign had lasted three years, until early 1050, when William was finally able to force the surrender of his rebellious cousin, Guy of Burgundy, who had fled with his troops and taken refuge in Brionne following his defeat in the battle at Val-es-Dunes in January 1047. During the long siege at Brionne, Lanfranc had given the duke not only physical succour but gifts William appreciated even more – spiritual comfort, wise counsel and friendship. Recognising extraordinary abilities when he saw them, William had enlisted Lanfranc as a special advisor and emissary. It was Lanfranc whom William had dispatched to Rome to persuade Pope Nicholas II to give a belated blessing to his marriage to Matilda. Lanfranc had been spectacularly successful in Rome.

Now the duke called Lanfranc again. From Caen, where the fifty-eight-year-old Lanfranc was now abbot of St Stephen's Abbey, William summoned him to the castle at Bonneville-sur-Touques. It was from the top of the stone tower of the Bonneville castle, near the mouth of the River Touques, that William sometimes gazed to the north, across the nearby countryside, over the rooftops and past the quays of Deauville and out upon the blue waters of the Channel, his mind filling with thoughts of the land and the enemy that lay beyond. William brought Lanfranc into his Bonneville castle and laid out his position and his plan.

In response, Lanfranc probably pointed out the crucial flaw in the duke's scheme to gain the Pope's support for a campaign to depose Harold: William didn't have a legal leg to stand on.

The duke would have demanded to know why not, and Lanfranc would have explained it. William was intending to assert a claim to the English crown based on: one, his designation by King Edward as his successor; and two, his blood kinship to the late Queen Emma, who was King Edward's mother and William's grandfather's sister. Fourteen years earlier, while Harold, his father and the rest of Godwin's family were out of favour, King Edward apparently had designated William as his successor. However, under English law and tradition, the king could not appoint his successor. He could name his choice, but he could not make him king. Under English law, the witan chose the king. So although King Edward had promised William that he would succeed Edward, William could not lawfully claim the crown on the basis of that promise. King Edward simply did not have the power to pass the crown to William.

In the matter of William's claim based on consanguinity, Lanfranc would have pointed out that Queen Emma was never in the line of succession to the English throne. She was queen by marriage alone. Her children and her grandchildren could rule if they were descended from either of her two husbands who had been England's king. But her relatives who were not descended from either of her husbands would have no legitimate claim. William's claim on that basis of consanguinity was not valid.

If William, feeling frustrated, wondered aloud whether Lanfranc was opposing him, Lanfranc would have told him that in this instance it was the truth that was opposing him. His advice to William was likely to be not to fight the truth, but instead to bring the truth to his side and make it his ally. He could do so by giving up the idea that he had a lawful claim to the English throne, since he didn't, and then finding other reasons for deposing Harold.

William was sure he had other reasons. Harold, he insisted, was a perjurer, a violator of oaths, a deceiver, a usurper, a man unfit to be king, a man with no background save an ambitious father. The Pope, Lanfranc may have told the duke, would be interested mainly in the spiritual and moral implications of Harold's being king. William's personal feelings, however understandable, would not be so significant in attempting to persuade his holiness to sanction the duke's venture.

William would have responded by telling Lanfranc that Harold had sworn before God and on holy relics that he would be William's liegeman, that he would represent William, that he would do all the things he had promised William. Was it possible, William might have asked, that the Pope could believe that a man who swore falsely before God, who dissembled before God, who defied the justice of God, a shamelessly self-seeking man, a man without honour, a violator of sacred oaths, was the man God willed to be king? Was he the man to rule over Church matters in England? Was he the man to serve the Church faithfully as steward of its treasures in England? Could such a man really be the man the Pope would wish in power in England?

Lanfranc would probably nod and say that his holiness would wish only what was best for the Church.

William perhaps would add to his list of allegations: Harold was a man of flagrantly corrupt morals, a fornicator who had brought children into the world without the benefit of a Church-sanctioned marriage; he lived openly with a woman who was not his wife; he lived in disdain for and in rebellion against the Church's requirements for a Christian family. Surely the Pope did not wish to have such a man as king of England.

Furthermore, William may have claimed, Stigand, the archbishop – or so-called archbishop – who supposedly heard King Edward designate Harold as his successor, was no more than Harold's family retainer. He was a fraudulent archbishop, illegally appointed while Robert of Jumièges, who was lawfully appointed, still held the office but was forced out of England by Harold and his father. Stigand was appointed solely at the demand of Harold's family, William might have claimed, in order to have him serve Harold's family's ends. The duke might have asked whether Stigand was an example of the Church appointments Harold could be expected to make. Could the Pope be willing to place into the hands of a morally corrupt self-server the future of the Church in England?

Lanfranc, familiar with the Church's affairs, might have offered some ammunition of his own. Harold and his brothers had persisted in supporting Stigand even though he was under a cloud of suspicion. Harold and his brothers had consistently resisted the reforms that Rome had asked the Church in England to make.

The duke and Lanfranc would agree, at least for the duke's purposes, that Harold was subversive to the Church's goals and that if left to his own devices he would allow, and even cause, great harm to befall the Church in England. It became clear that Lanfranc's unavoidable duty was to inform the Pope of the danger. If the Pope deemed them proper, he would need to take appropriate measures.

Lanfranc's mission, then, assigned to him by Duke William, was to make certain that the Pope deemed measures proper. It was perhaps then that Lanfranc let the duke know that his holiness, Pope Alexander II, had been a student of his at Le Bec. Lanfranc knew his holiness well. And perhaps it was after that that William let Lanfranc know that once the crown of England was William's, he thought Lanfranc would make an outstanding archbishop.

10

THE PREPARATIONS
FEBRUARY 1066–APRIL 1066

T he conference, believed to be the first such assembly ever
held in Normandy, was held in Duke William's sprawling castle at Lillebonne, where the Seine flowed into the sea. The
ancient city had once been a Roman capital, a major metropolis, then
known as Juliobona, named in honour of the Roman general whose
armies had conquered Gaul, Julius Caesar. In 1066 it still bore signs of
its Roman era, including the ruins of the 10,000-seat theatre that the
Romans had built there.

The conference had been ordered by Duke William and in atten-
dance were virtually all of his nobles and close allies, the men whose
help he had to have if he was to amass an army powerful enough to
face King Harold with a chance of success.

It was February; there on the south shore of the Channel there were
already hints of spring in the air, and William was feeling a growing
urgency to get on with the job of building a powerful invasion force.
When he addressed his audience, however, it wasn't a matter of his simply commanding his barons to ante up the troops he needed; he had to
sell them the idea of an invasion, since their obligation to provide him
with fighting men did not include service beyond the borders of France.
They had no duty to follow their duke to the other side of the Channel.
And so he would take them, as it were, up on the mountaintop, where he

could show them all that he saw. He wanted to share his grand view of what he tried to make seem a veritable promised land. He apparently believed that they would respond appropriately.

Instead they responded with hard questions, criticism and restive murmurs that revealed their deep doubts about the duke's proposal. They begged off from commitments, saying they needed more time to think about it. The general assembly disintegrated into small groups, in which the complaints and misgivings were even more strongly stated. Some were for the idea, saying they were eager to follow the duke to England. Others argued the impossibility of success, refusing to co-operate. The arguments for and against participation grew both fierce and emotional.

William fitz Osbern stepped in to try to recapture control. He met with the groups and pleaded for their loyalty. Heads began to shake. The opposition was wide and firm. Many of the nobles were frank in saying that they believed an attempt to conquer England was a hope-less venture doomed to fail. Those who believed there was a chance of success thought that it was so small that the potential gain was not worth risking either their own lives or those of their men. Fitz Osbern was sympathetic, so much so that the barons asked him to convey their true feelings to the duke, which he consented to do. He would, they thought, speak on their behalf, presenting their legitimate concerns to Duke William. He would also, they no doubt hoped, take the heat of the duke's wrath for them.

When the entire group reassembled in the great hall, in the presence of the duke, fitz Osbern began to speak. He declared the love and loy-alty of the duke's noblemen and promised that they would not merely support the duke's campaign but would contribute double the number of fighting men that they were ordinarily required to provide. The nobles, realising they had been betrayed by fitz Osbern, instantly rose in outrage, their protests so loud that no clear voice could be heard in the vast chamber. The hall exploded into a clamour. Duke William angrily adjourned the meeting until later, perhaps until the next day.

The duke hastily devised a new stratagem. Putting the barons of Normandy all together in one room where they could gang up on him, where they could be brave in front of the others, had been a big mistake, he could see. His new tactic was to divide them and pick them off one by one.

The barons were quietly summoned individually to face him. With William sat a clerk with quill, ink and a ledger. The duke flattered and cajoled each, made vague promises and told each one what others were contributing to the campaign. He then solicited a pledge of specific support from each one. Their pledges were recorded by the clerk. Odo, perhaps acting as a shill, promised to contribute one hundred ships and enough fighting men to fill them. Robert of Mortain, the duke's other half-brother, promised 120 ships and the men to go with them. Count Robert of Eu pledged sixty ships, and men, as did William fitz Osbern. The list grew. Hugh of Avranches pledged sixty ships, and men; Hugh of Montfort, fifty ships, and men; Bishop Remigius one ship, and men; Nicholas, the abbot of St Ouen, twenty ships, and men; Gerald Dapifer, forty ships, and men. Richard, count of Evreux, eighty ships, and men. Roger of Montgomery and Roger of Beaumont each pledged sixty ships, and men. Both Walter Giffard and Vulgrin, the bishop of Le Mans, pledged thirty ships, and men. By the end of his series of personal meetings, each of the assembled nobles had given William a pledge of specific support, all recorded in the duke's ledger. Together they had balked at joining the duke's expedition; separately, defeated by the force of the duke's personality, they had officially signed on.

Now, for the first time since he had sworn he would go to England and seize the crown from Harold, William had a valid estimate of the strength of his invasion force.

It fell short of what he wanted, less than what he believed he needed. He needed more than what the ledger told him he would have coming. When he voiced that judgement to his advisors, someone is likely to have reminded him that Normandy had just so many men and that they were sending out recruiters to hire mercenaries, as he had instructed.

The need was for big numbers, the duke probably responded, not just a man here and there. Big numbers, however, were likely to require taking on big partners and making big promises. William would consider doing whatever it took. Flanders and Denmark both should be willing to help. He gave instructions to contact them. He also ordered a meeting to be arranged between himself and King Philip of France.

The duke also wanted his advisors to find men who knew the English coast, experts who knew every foot of coastline from Weymouth to Dover. He wanted them to come up with possible landing sites. They were to consider: one, the site must be reasonably close to the Norman port of embarkation; the duke didn't want to spend any more time in the crossing than he absolutely had to. Two, the site had to have a beach or other terrain that the duke's army could negotiate easily; he didn't want to have to scale bluffs or slog through marsh or hack his way through brush. Three, the site must be away from fortifications; the duke didn't want to have to fight and lose a lot of men just to get ashore. Four, the site had to be defensible; once they were ashore, he wanted to be able to establish a base that he could secure and hold indefinitely. And five, the site had to be extensive enough that his troops and horses could survive on nearby forage.

William would want to know all the advantages and disadvantages of each possible site. When he knew all that, he would be in a position to pick one of them. He very likely emphasised to his top advisors that he wanted maximum thought and care put into the landing site selection. The landing site would be absolutely crucial. They had to get it right.

Harold received William's message sent via William Malet. In a meeting with Malet, presumably in the palace at Westminster, Harold listened to what the duke had instructed Malet to say. Then he gave Malet an answer to be delivered to the duke. The exact words are unknown, but the drift of the message was that Harold, now the lawful king of England, had no intention of abdicating his high office and he rejected any claim that Duke William might make.

If Malet spoke what was on the duke's mind, he would have pointedly asked if Harold was repudiating the solemn oaths he had sworn to Duke William, before God and on holy relics.

Harold, responding, would explain that those promises were made under duress and any fair-minded person would recognise that a man isn't to be held to promises he was forced to make or pledges not freely given. The law, he would point out, so provided. Perhaps it was then that Harold told Malet there was one promise he would keep. Duke William had asked Harold to give his little sister to one of the duke's barons to marry. Harold instructed Malet to tell the duke that unfortunately Harold's sister had died about a year earlier, but if the duke and his baron still wanted her, Harold would send him her remains.

The meeting with Malet was then ended.

Harold must have realised all along, even before his trip to Normandy, that there was a possibility of an invasion attempt by

William. Now he felt entirely certain that an invasion would come. He would confer with his brothers Gyrth and Leofwine, who were his closest confidants and his chief lieutenants. He would count on them to provide not only a substantial part of his fighting force but leadership and counsel as well. With his brothers, he now began making preparations in earnest.

As king, Harold would command an army comprising three categories of fighting men. One category, the backbone of the military service, was the housecarls, the full-time professional soldiers, on the payroll of the king or of an earl. They were highly trained, disciplined and fully equipped fighting men, the elite cadre of England's armed force, able to fight on land and sea. Harold had his royal housecarls, plus those of Wessex, over which he was, in effect, still earl. Gyrth and Leofwine had the housecarls of their earldoms, as did Edwin and Morkere. In times of national emergency, earls were expected to contribute their housecarls to serve in the king's army, which became the nation's army. Altogether, they numbered perhaps 3,500 men.

The two other categories were composed of conscripts, and together they made up the fyrd, the king's part-time army. One group was the territorial muster, the quota of fighting men owed by thanes to the earl – or, in some cases, the bishop – through whom the thane held his estate. Thanes were required by law to provide one soldier – mounted, armed and equipped with helmet and byrnie – for each five hides of land in their estate. A hide was roughly the amount of land necessary to support one family, and the actual size varied. The fighting men of the territorial muster were provided, by their thanes, with enough provisions and pay to last two months.

The other group of the fyrd – and the third category of fighting men – was the mass levy, which included every able-bodied freeman between the ages of sixteen and fifty, whether a property owner or not. Every such freeman – slaves were exempt – owed the king military service, and freemen constituted by far the largest, but least capable and least equipped, part of the king's army. Although obligated for two months' service a year, either in construction or in combat, they were rarely called to fight. The king did use them, however, to build bridges and fortifications. Men of the fyrd were required to serve either on land or at sea, one or the other, unlike housecarls, who were expected to fight on both land *and* sea.

The numerical strength of the fyrd was difficult to measure, not even the king knowing precise numbers, but the territorial muster was estimated at about 10,000 men and the mass levy as high as 50,000 men.

Unlike the armies of other nations of western Europe, England's was an army of foot soldiers, horses being used not as cavalry mounts, as Norman chevaliers used them, but simply as transportation to carry men and equipment to the field of battle. The English soldier's favourite weapons were: the two-handed, single-headed battleaxe with a heavy, convexly curved blade, a brutally murderous instrument of war adopted from the Danes; the Saxon sword, which had a straight, slightly tapered, pointed, double-edged steel blade, about thirty-three inches long, down most of the length of which, on both sides of the blade, ran a fuller, to lighten the weight of the sword, with a short, curved handguard between blade and grip and a pommel at the end of the grip, and carried in a fleece-lined scabbard, the oiliness of the fleece helping to protect the blade from rust; and the spear, its twelve-inch-long, leaf-shaped, sharply pointed steel head mounted on a seven-foot-long ash shaft, suitable for throwing like a javelin, or stabbing, and used in hunting as well as in warfare.

The English army also included archers, their bows four to five feet long, their arrows carried in a quiver at the waist, their skill earning them status as special troops. Men from the mass levy, most of them merely fighting farmers, were likely to be lightly armed, their weapons no more than staves, clubs and crude maces made of sticks and stones.

The shields carried by the housecarls and the fyrdmen of the territorial muster, some round, some kite-shaped, were made with a wood frame, banded by a steel rim, covered with tough leather and held with a handgrip inside the metal boss at the centre of the shield. Standard combat tactics of the English army called for deployment of troops in the traditional Saxon shield wall, the armoured warriors – housecarls and men of the territorial muster – standing shoulder to shoulder in a line several ranks deep, shields before them, facing the enemy. In combat, men armed with battleaxes slung their shields over their shoulders by means of leather straps, freeing both hands to wield the heavy, long-handled axe. The shield wall had proved effective against many foes, over many years of Anglo-Saxon warfare. It was the way of fighting that the English knew and liked best.

England also had a navy, which would be the nation's first line of defence against an enemy force coming by sea. Harold and his brothers, like their father before them, had their own private fleets to protect the coasts of their earldoms and their other interests, and in addition Harold, as king, commanded the Royal Navy, a full-time force of professional fighting sailors. Five of the nation's most strategic and most vulnerable port cities, the so-called Cinque Ports – Dover, Sandwich, Romney, Hastings and Hythe – maintained their own small navies under an arrangement they had made with the late King Edward, and their ships, twenty from each of the five cities, each ship manned by a steersman and twenty-one crewmen, were available to King Harold.

Those combined naval forces, totalling perhaps 200 ships, were augmented by the naval fyrd. England's magnates, secular and clerical alike, were required by law to contribute toward the national defence one ship and a crew of sixty armed oarsmen for each 300 hides of land within their estate. Altogether, the English naval force, full-time and part-time, might number as many as 400 vessels and crews.

The ships of the English fleet were built following the Viking longship model, open boats powered by oars and a single, square sail. Some of the ships were more than seventy feet long and capable of carrying as many as 140 men. The tactics of war at sea were no more advanced than what they were in Caesar's time, a thousand years earlier. If Harold's navy was to stop or hinder William's invaders, the English ships would have to close on the Norman vessels, come alongside and send their fighting crewmen over the gunwales and into the enemy ships, engaging William's troops, huddled as passengers aboard their sail-powered transports, in bloody, close-quarter combat, hacking, stabbing and bludgeoning away till the battle was decided, ship by ship.

The biggest question Harold and his advisors had to try to answer was: where would William come? Another was nearly as big: *when* would he come? If Harold knew precisely where, the when wouldn't matter so much. Knowing the where, he could concentrate his forces on the place of assault and simply wait, rotating troops and seamen in and out at that one spot. He had enough men to do that. As it was, however, he knew neither when nor where William would come and so he was forced to spread out his forces along practically the entire southern coast of England. That required many more men. He would have to call out enough of the fyrd to position troops at all those possible landing points simultaneously. That would place a mammoth demand on manpower.

His other major consideration, a huge one, was the timing of the muster of the fyrd. He had to be careful that he didn't muster the fyrd too soon, or their service time would expire before the Normans arrived. It was an enormous guessing game, in which a wrong guess could easily be fatal.

To speculation that William might come before summer, Harold is likely to have answered that he doubted that he would. William would need the wind and the weather with him, and if he came before summer, they would likely be against him. Besides, Harold would realise, William needed time to put together an army, a massive force. He would need ships, too, Harold would realise, and he would probably have to build or borrow most of what he needed. That would require time also.

Summer was perhaps the best guess Harold, his brothers and other advisors could make. Their speculation as to *where* was another matter entirely, perhaps no better defined than 'God only knows'.

At the earliest time of preparation, January or February probably, Harold perhaps planned to begin calling out the fyrd in July, by shires, and to post them at all the most likely landing sites, perhaps from Portland all the way to the mouth of the Thames. He would plan a naval defence as well. His seamen would have two objectives: to engage ships of the invasion fleet and kill as many of William's troops as they could before the Normans reached shore; and to prevent William's ships from landing where they intended to, forcing them to alter their course in order to avoid the English ships. Harold's forces would try to prevent William from following his plan, whatever it was.

Harold was making the long trip from Westminster to York with more than one objective in mind. His first objective was to win the recalcitrant Northumbrians over to his side and have their witan endorse him as their king, so that he would indeed be king of all England, not merely of the rest of it. The second objective was to fulfil, with whatever reluctance he felt, his promise to Edwin and Morkere to make their sister, Alditha, his queen, an act crucial to the first objective. A third objective was the recruitment of Mercia's and Northumbria's armies, housecarls and fyrds, in defence against the coming Norman invasion.

In York his meeting with the members of the witan perhaps went better than Harold had expected. He had taken with him to York an old friend and confidant, the widely respected and saintly bishop of Worcester, Wulfstan. The bishop's counsel and his presence at the meetings where Harold spoke to the Northumbrian witan helped Harold win the witan's acceptance. The bishop sat at Harold's side during the meetings, as did Earl Morkere, in a public show of support. Wulfstan had urged Harold to address the concerns of the Northumbrians, to be sincere and straightforward, but firm as well, and Harold followed his advice. By the time the meetings concluded, after nearly a week of sometimes turbulent sessions, and with Wulfstan himself having delivered an earnest, get-right-with-the-Lord-and-with-your-king sermon, Harold had been acknowledged by the Northumbrian nobles as their king.

Then came the time for the wedding.

Lady Alditha Aelfgarsdottir was probably about eighteen years old when her father, the late erratic earl of Mercia, sought to buy peace with his troublesome neighbour to the west, the fiery and defiant king of Wales, Griffith ap Llewellyn, by giving her to him as his wife. Now, nearly nine years later, in the waning winter of 1066, she was about twenty-six, a widow for almost three years and living with her young daughter, her only child, on an estate owned by her brother Edwin, earl of Mercia.

Her brothers no doubt sought her co-operation by specifying the advantages of being the wife of the king of England. In the end, of course, she agreed to do her part in the deal that Edwin and Morkere had worked out with Harold, and, perhaps with some eagerness, she awaited the new king's coming for her.

The wedding ceremony was to be held at York Cathedral, presided over by Archbishop Eldred. Harold presumably wanted it kept as simple as possible and to keep the celebration that must follow the ceremony as short as possible. He probably didn't feel like celebrating at all, but he would do what was necessary to make it a proper royal wedding in the eyes of Edwin and Morkere and their Mercian and Northumbrian constituents.

The ceremony was held at mid-morning, to allow ample time for the celebration to follow. During the ceremony, before an audience of witnesses that overflowed the grand old cathedral, the archbishop prayed that the couple would be united in love and in service to God, and that God would bless their sacred union with offspring, granting, as put by the words of Genesis 49:26, which the archbishop quoted, 'blessings of the breasts and of the womb'.

The celebration at Morkere's palace would continue into the evening, the men having gathered in one of the palace halls, the women in another. Sometime during the evening Harold would excuse himself to the Aelfgarson brothers and rise to leave the hall, which is likely to have remained filled with boisterous voices and drunken laughter.

Lady Alditha was waiting for him in his chambers. She perhaps then thanked him warmly for her dower gift, a manor she could now call her very own. Whatever he was feeling, which very likely included intoxication, he would realise that she was now his legal wife, and the agreement with her brothers called for his acting as a husband to her. He was expected to consummate the marriage now. Alditha knew what was expected of her and she doubtless wanted to give him a happy wedding night. She also wanted, presumably, her morning gift, the traditional present that English bridegrooms gave their brides the morning after, to show their appreciation for a grand start to their connubiality. A proper husband would give his bride an opportunity to gain his gratitude, and a generous morning gift to show that she had succeeded.

So the evening passed.

Sometime later, Harold met again with Edwin and Morkere. The talk now was about Harold's defence plan. The Aelfgarson brothers, however, indicated more concern with defending an attack coming across the North Sea than with one from across the English Channel. They likely had heard reports of Tostig's attempts to raise an army and, from where they sat, the prospect of an invasion by Tostig was more worrisome than a possible invasion by Duke William. Edwin and Morkere may have had doubts about Harold's willingness to defend Northumbria and Mercia with the same vigour as he would Wessex.

If so, Harold would assure them that a threat to Northumbria and Mercia was a threat to the king and to England, no matter from whom it came or whence it came. Northumbria was England as much as Wessex was. The king and England's armed forces under his command, he would make clear, would defend Northumbria and Mercia against *any* foreign attack.

It was perhaps then that the Aelfgarson brothers pledged their support in the defence against Duke William and his Norman army. Harold took the next couple of weeks to travel throughout Northumbria, the new queen and Bishop Wulfstan riding beside him as he made courtesy calls on Northumbrian nobles and let himself be seen and heard by villagers and farmers. The trip was part of a public relations campaign suggested by Wulfstan and it apparently won for King Harold a new degree of acceptance in Northumbria. It was the first time that a king of England had travelled that far north since King Canute and his army marched through Northumbria in 1017.

Returning to York, Harold then gathered up his retinue and headed south, back toward London.

There was business to be taken care of there. The government was not at a standstill while the king took a wife and made preparations for war. Harold had already repealed some laws that, when an earl, he had thought burdensome or unnecessary and he was considering others for repeal or amendment. He was a strict law-and-order ruler, not for the mere sake of obedience to the law but for the sake of protection for the people, and he issued directives to his reeves, earls and thanes to enforce the laws and assure the protection of all within their jurisdictions, particularly from robbery, theft and disturbance of the peace. He believed that all citizens were entitled to live in peaceful enjoyment of their lives and property, and he urged his law enforcement and judicial officers to make sure they were allowed to do so. He was determined to be regarded by the people as a friend of the good, especially including the clergy, God's special servants, and a stern foe of those whose deeds were evil. He also attempted to promote trade and general prosperity throughout the realm by ordering new coinage minted and quickly placed in circulation. The new coins, which he had had designed, bore his likeness, the royal crown upon his head, on the obverse, and the Latin 'Pax' on the reverse. There were also appointments to be decided upon and made, such as the one needed for the abbey at Abingdon, whose abbot had recently died, and for the abbey at Ely, which was being transferred from Archbishop Stigand's holdings.

But mainly his thoughts and his time doubtlessly were unavoidably absorbed by the national defence plans, which by mid-April had become firm and were at the early stages of implementation. In a meeting at the Westminster palace Harold gave the national witan a full briefing on what his intelligence agents had reported to him from Normandy, what he expected from William, and what his plans were to defend the nation. He also told them of the possible threat from Tostig and whatever foreign ally Tostig might bring to his side.

The strange and awesome star, which seemed to have flaming hair streaming from its head, was first observed in February, though few had seen it then, much less made something of it. But it had grown brighter with each passing week, until in the week following Easter, 16 April, the week that followed Harold's meeting with the witan, it compelled its notice by all. It was a fearsome sight, moving southward each night across the dark sky, glowing far brighter than any other star, seeming closer than any other, lighting the sky from dusk till dawn, coming out of nowhere, going only God knew where. Surely it was an omen, a dreadful portent of some unthinkable catastrophe to come, a clear and awful warning from God, the God of Heaven and of Earth, who both the stars in their paths and the destiny of Earth's kings does ordain.

Actually the comet being seen over all of Europe had been observed and remarked upon by Chinese students of the heavens some thirteen centuries earlier, and it had appeared with predictable regularity every seventy-five years since then. In later years it would come to be called Halley's Comet. But in that week after Easter in 1066 it was a frightening, portentous event.

Harold had seen it. Duke William had seen it. All over Europe everyone capable of concocting a theory concerning it had seen it, as had everyone else with sightful eyes. It was inescapably conspicuous and it had spawned a hundred explanations, perhaps more. Many of the explanations had become part of daily conversation in England, and elsewhere. The strange star was a sign of something terrible to come, everyone agreed, but exactly what was it that was to happen? About that question there was a great deal of controversy.

Many experts of the day said that it heralded the advent of a new king, like the star over Bethlehem. Many others said it presaged disaster, such as the Viking invasions. If it signalled a new king, the question then arose, was the king Harold? Or someone else? If it forecast a coming disaster, would it be disaster for England? Or Normandy?

No one could yet say for sure.

II

THE PAPAL DECISION
SPRING 1066

G ilbert of Lisieux was the man Lanfranc chose, with Duke
William's approval, for the mission to Rome. Earnest, stu-
dious, quiet-spoken but eloquent, in his late thirties, per-
sonable and likeable, Gilbert was archdeacon of the diocese of Lisieux,
second-in-command to the bishop and, in Lanfranc's opinion, a
comer.

Perhaps Lanfranc wrote out the charges against King Harold, in
addition to detailing them to Gilbert orally. Lanfranc would want
Gilbert to be completely familiar with them, so that he could speak as
one who was personally knowledgeable. The points he was to drive
home were that Duke William was going to England out of his concern for the welfare of the Church there; he was going to preserve and
protect the Church and its holy mission; he was going as God's agent.
Therefore, as God's agent, he both deserved and needed the blessing of
the Church and of its holy father, the Pope. Gilbert's ultimate objective
was to have the Pope declare the duke's expedition to be a holy crusade, a cause sanctioned by the Church.

Gilbert was to paint King Harold as an immoralist, a usurper, a
heretic, a pernicious influence on the English people and on
Christianity, a rebel against the true Church and a danger to the Pope
as well as a threat to the Church. If during his briefing Gilbert asked

Lanfranc whether Harold was indeed all that bad, Lanfranc likely would have told him his job was to make him seem so in the eyes of Rome.

Furthermore, Gilbert was to have the Pope understand the advantages of making a political alliance with William. The Pope needed strong friends, and his granting of William and Lanfranc's requests would gain him a friend who, in the years to come, Gilbert would promise, would gladly show his gratitude for the Pope's support. The Pope should be able to recognise the political as well as the spiritual advantages.

Gilbert's instructions, which he no doubt committed to his memory during his three-week journey, called for him, following his arrival in Rome, to present his letters of introduction from Duke William and Lanfranc and seek first of all an audience not with the Pope but with the man whom those in the know regarded as the most influential person in Church headquarters. That man was Hildebrand, archdeacon of the Rome diocese, a man many thought would one day be Pope himself (they were later proved correct). The bishop of Rome, Hildebrand's immediate superior, to whom he had easy access, was of course the Pope.

Forty-two years old, small, spidery, made conspicuous by his odd looks, Hildebrand was a German Benedictine monk who by intellect, strength of will, force of personality, righteous zeal and unmixed confidence in the correctness of his view of the truth, had risen speedily through the complex hierarchy of the Church. He had managed to insinuate himself into an extraordinary position of power behind the papal throne. As an ardent (some of his colleagues interpreted his German name as *hellbrand*, 'pure flame') servant of the Church, he had formed priorities that he doggedly pursued on behalf of the Church. They tended to fall into one of only two categories: spiritual and political. But they were all combined in his singular, overriding purpose: to enhance the welfare of the Church.

The Church, he believed, was suffering from, among other things, too much power by German kings, who claimed to be successors to the emperors of the long-fallen Roman empire and who ruled northern Italy as well as Germany, a territory and political entity that history writers would later call the Holy Roman Empire, though neither holy nor Roman. German kings, the emperors of the Holy Roman Empire, had been dictating the selection of Popes, which Hildebrand saw as an intolerable abuse and a danger to the Church. He was determined that the power to name the Pope would be taken from them and placed in the hands of the cardinals of the Church. The Church's business was for churchmen to conduct, not laymen, not even if they were kings or emperors.

In Hildebrand's view, all temporal powers, including those of nations, governments and rulers, were derived from God. Therefore nations and governments should logically be united under God and supervised by God's earthly representatives – the Church and its leader, the Pope. Authority over kings and nations, he believed, rightly belonged to the Pope, God's chief overseer on Earth.

Hildebrand was also a stickler for sexual rectitude, lapses of which by its priests had created problems for the Church and diminished its moral stature. Hildebrand insisted that sexual appetites be reined in and that priests practice celibacy and abstinence – notions widely challenged by those clerics who kept wives or concubines, or both, and the children they had had by them. The strict views of Hildebrand regarding sexual conduct had become widely known among the clergy who kept up with Church affairs, men such as Abbot Lanfranc.

Gilbert was received warmly by Hildebrand. Speaking in Latin, the language of the Church, the two men soon got down to business. Gilbert begged Hildebrand's help and that of the holy father in marshalling the forces of the Lord Jesus and His Church to assist Duke William in a righteous and pressing cause. Hildebrand, of course, wasn't exactly uninformed about William's intentions concerning England, news of such an endeavour being difficult to contain.

Hildebrand probably let Gilbert know that he had been concerned about the condition of the Church in England for some time. One of the things about it that bothered him was English churchmen's insistence on writing in their own language instead of the Church's language. The English clergy were notorious for speaking and writing in English. Their doing so evidently indicated a deplorably bad attitude.

Gilbert would eagerly inform Hildebrand about King Harold. He was, Gilbert might have begun, striking home with his first thrust, an open and shameless adulterer. Then Gilbert would heap up and embellish the charges that William and Lanfranc had conjured up.

Hildebrand would indicate he was prepared to support Duke William's petition to the holy father and to the papal court, but he would undoubtedly want to know something of the duke's plans if William were to be successful in defeating King Harold.

Now Gilbert would show he was deserving of Lanfranc's confidence. He would portray Duke William as having legitimate claims to England's crown and perhaps claim that were it not for the perfidy of Harold, the duke's accession to the English throne would have already been accomplished, in an orderly manner, without violence, without bloodshed, without loss of Christian lives. After all, that was what the late King Edward, that saint of God, had wanted for England and for Duke William, who was King Edward's kinsman and his designated successor, a wish thwarted, temporarily, by the pretender and usurper, Harold.

The duke, already a strong and generous friend of the Church, Gilbert would say, would of course receive the benefit of additional resources when he became king of England and was placed in the position of influence over the Church in England. The additional ways that Duke William would be able to aid the Church and advance its purposes were incalculable, but obviously many and great.

Naturally the placement of the duke in that high position, allowing him authority over all the rich resources of England and of the Church in England, would add to the resources of the Church in Rome and worldwide. The duke's intent, Hildebrand was assured, was to hold those resources, hold that authority, not for William's own use but for the cause of the Lord Jesus Christ and for the Church that Christ ordained to serve his holy cause. The duke's victory would be the victory of the Lord Jesus Christ and His Church.

What Hildebrand would want to know then was whether, if the holy father were to grant his blessing, Duke William would agree to hold the English crown under the lordship of the holy father. Gilbert evidently assured Hildebrand that he would, that Duke William would become the liegeman of the Pope (a promise that William would much later repudiate).

By the time the convening of the papal court was arranged, Hildebrand, with Gilbert apparently beside him, had already thoroughly briefed his holiness, Pope Alexander II, the former Anselm, bishop of Lucca, and Lanfranc's former student. Before the court, which would debate the question of papal support for Duke William's invasion of England, Hildebrand would make the major presentation.

An assistant would make the arrangements for the convening of the court, notifying all concerned and giving them adequate time to research the matter and inform themselves. To whatever question the assistant asked concerning provisions and accommodations for those who would represent King Harold and present his case to the court, the response was, in effect, 'Don't bother. There will be no representatives of King Harold.' It was to be a one-sided argument.

Following a long, impassioned debate, during which Hildebrand proved an effective champion of the duke's cause, the papal court decided in favour of Duke William. The Pope then pronounced the duke's campaign against Harold a holy crusade, the cause of righteousness against evil. Gilbert returned to Rouen bearing not only the great good news but the papal banner, white with a red cross, which the Pope had given him to present to Duke William, allowing the duke to go to war beneath the symbol of the Church's authorisation.

Gilbert also carried to the duke another gift from the Pope, a heavy gold ring blessed by the holy father and containing, in a tiny compartment covered by the hinged, engraved top of the ring, one of the most sacred relics the Pope could give, an enormously powerful token of divine favour to be borne by the duke into battle – a hair believed to be from the holy head of St Peter himself.

12

THE BETRAYAL

SPRING 1066

Count Conan of Brittany had no intention of giving any sort of assistance to the Bastard's plans for the invasion of England. The count had his own invasion plans. First he would deal with Anjou, the French county that bordered Brittany on the south-east. Once he had taken it, he would be in a better position to move on Maine, Normandy's ally, bordering Anjou, Brittany and Normandy. Then he would move against Normandy itself, which he insisted was rightfully his, not the Bastard's, since Conan was the *legitimate* great-grandson of Richard I, duke of Normandy, through the line of Richard's daughter Hawise, who had married Geoffrey, duke of Brittany, Conan's grandfather.

His chances of success in any hostile move toward Normandy would be infinitely increased by the absence of William and, better still, by the absence of a huge part of William's fighting force. So Conan was all for William's invasion of England. With a little bit of luck, he figured, the Bastard would get himself killed over there. Even if he didn't, the void that William would leave in Normandy while he was gone would allow Conan to sweep in and take over. Conan likely was thinking that even if William managed to make it back from England, he wouldn't be strong enough, after fighting the English – whether he won or lost – to displace Conan.

The problem for Conan was that William apparently had guessed, or had received intelligence on, what he was planning.

From his castle in Rennes, Conan set out on a march to besiege Angers, in western Anjou, on the Loire River. He was on horseback, holding the leather reins in a leather-gloved hand, carrying his shield in his other hand, also gloved. Sometime during the siege, perhaps soon after eating, Conan was mysteriously stricken and fell dead. Some said later his heart had simply given out. Others were certain he had been poisoned. One theory had it that a deadly concentrate, perhaps from one of the nightshade plants, belladonna or henbane, had been applied to his reins and gloves and he had ingested it when he put his hands to his mouth. The theory had it that Duke William was the instigator.

Whatever the explanation, Count Conan of Brittany was dead. A dangerous thorn had been removed from the figurative side of Duke William and the literal side of Normandy.

By an odd twist of circumstances, Duke William was a kinsman of Harold's brother Tostig. Tostig's wife, Judith, was the half-sister of Baldwin V, the count of Flanders. Matilda, William's wife, was Baldwin's daughter. Judith was therefore Matilda's aunt, and Tostig was Matilda's uncle by marriage. By Matilda's marriage, Tostig was also uncle to William. The relationship, however, meant little or nothing to the duke.

It did, though, put the two men on speaking terms. Tostig would have little difficulty arranging a meeting with the duke in Rouen. At it he offered a proposition to William. He told William that they had a common goal, that both of them wished to claim their rights in England and that they had a common foe, Harold, standing in the way. Tostig said he could help William get what he wanted, that he had men and ships and a good record as a general.

Men and ships were what William was looking for. But before he got into the specifics of how many men, how many ships, he likely wanted to find out what Tostig hoped to get out of an arrangement, if there were to be one. William had an idea of what Tostig could do for him; he wanted to know what he could do for Tostig. Whatever his ultimate aspirations were, Tostig is likely to have replied that he wanted Northumbria back.

It would be an alliance hard to imagine as working satisfactorily. Through Matilda's family, William knew enough about Tostig and his stormy personality to know that the first time William crossed him or in any way thwarted his plans, Tostig's temper would go up like Greek fire. William perhaps also figured that a man who would betray his own brother would even more easily betray his ally, given a reason. It would be dangerous, foolhardy even, to trust that kind of man. Whatever Tostig had to offer in the way of fighting men and ships, William evidently decided, it wasn't worth the trouble, let alone the danger, of dealing with Tostig. He turned Tostig down.

The duke's refusal to support his cause was Tostig's second rebuff. He had first tried King Sweyn of Denmark. Sweyn was his cousin, the son of Tostig's uncle, Ulf, who was Tostig's mother's brother. Sweyn's mother was Estrith, the sister of Canute, who had been king of England, Norway and Denmark at the same time. Cousin Sweyn, Tostig reasoned, had a legitimate claim to the English throne and all Tostig had to do was stimulate Sweyn's interest in pursuing it. Sweyn had an army and a navy and enough other resources, Tostig estimated, to have a chance of overthrowing Harold. Once they had beaten Harold, Tostig apparently had told Sweyn, if running two countries was more than Sweyn wanted to take on, he could stay in Denmark and rule it, and Tostig would stay in England and rule it in Sweyn's name, as his viceroy.

Sweyn hadn't bought it, deciding that he had enough problems keeping himself on the Danish throne, considering the lingering threat of attack by King Harald of Norway.

Now, after two rejections, his anger smouldering, Tostig was deciding what he would do next.

Atop the tall cliffs on the south-western shore of the Isle of Wight, Harold's officers had posted coast guards. They had been alertly gazing out upon the Channel's waters through sunshine and gloom, waiting and watching for the appearance of Norman ships bearing armed invaders. The wind had shifted only days before, now coming from the south-west, increasing the danger of a Norman invasion, and on this May morning what the coast guards saw set their hearts pounding. The breeze was carrying a fleet of single-sail vessels past their view, moving diagonally from their right to left, bearing toward the beaches on the south-eastern shore of the arrowhead-shaped island.

By the time the invaders started coming ashore, their longboats run up onto the sandy beaches east of Shanklin, it was obvious they were not Duke William's Norman army. Their leader was certainly no Norman. He had grown up near this place and was well known on the island. He was Tostig Godwinson.

Arrayed behind him was his small army of English, Flemish and Norman mercenaries and dozens of English expatriates who had thrown in with him, a thousand or more fighting men all told. He had come to offer the men of the Isle of Wight an opportunity to join him in a fight to depose Harold. If they refused, which they did, he would give them an opportunity to hand over their treasures and provisions – or give up their lives.

Then, as suddenly as they had come, Tostig and his army left, their plunder loaded aboard their ships.

From the Isle of Wight, with the prevailing wind still blowing from the south-west, Tostig's fleet sailed eastward along the Wessex coast on a voyage that Tostig had made once before. Fourteen years earlier, in 1052, he had sailed with his brothers and father on a voyage to force their way back into England, stopping at ports along the Wessex and Sussex coasts and going ashore to rally Earl Godwin's supporters and enlist them in an army that would confront King Edward at the gates of London. That voyage had been immensely successful, having led to the restoration of Earl Godwin's title, lands, wealth and power. Tostig now was expecting a similar response from the people of Wessex, evidently believing, for whatever reason or for none at all, that they preferred him over Harold. He apparently envisioned entire towns turning out to celebrate his coming and to join his campaign. With such massive support as he imagined, he planned to confront Harold in the same way his father had confronted King Edward, with comparable results.

His first stop after the disappointing experience on the Isle of Wight was Selsey, where, this time, he went in less threateningly, leaving the main body of his force lying offshore. The reception, however, was the same. His call for volunteers to enlist in his cause was met by stunned silence at first, then mild protest.

His demands were also the same. Men or money. Helpless before a thousand armed men, the residents of Selsey turned over their money and provisions.

Tostig and his followers then quickly withdrew and sailed on, skipping from town to town along the coast, from Selsey to Shoreham to Brighton to Pevensey to Hastings to Romney to Dover to Sandwich, and places in between. At each stop he met rebuff, till finally he began to accept the truth. Rallying the men of Wessex to his side was a vain hope, wholly unrealistic. Realisation of the truth moved him to deeper feelings of frustration and anger.

At Shoreham he went ashore in full force, threatening to overwhelm the town and demanding tribute. At Pevensey he demanded not only money and supplies but hostages, which he took with him, young men whom he could press into service. He set towns and farms afire, allowing his troops to pillage, rape and murder in what became savage hit-and-run raids.

At Sandwich, home port of the royal fleet, Tostig's little armada sailed boldly into the harbour in a surprise attack and in a short, bloody battle seized the town and the ships that lay anchored there. By that startling victory, Tostig won a foothold, in a vital and strategic location.

In the palace at Westminster, Harold was receiving reports of Tostig's depredations and atrocities. Efforts to combat Tostig had so far failed, his hit-and-run tactics having precluded the massing of an army of housecarls to engage him and his mercenaries. Harold was reluctant to call out the fyrd so early in the year, though doing so would give him the numbers he needed to defend the coast against Tostig. He was thinking of the greater threat of the Norman invasion and the time limit on the fyrdmen's service.

Whatever Tostig's plan was, Harold realised he must stop him now. He ordered out his housecarls and prepared to march to Sandwich, there to confront and repel Tostig's army of mercenaries. It was a sixty-five-mile march to Sandwich, through Rochester and Canterbury, and by the time he reached it, Harold figured, he would have an overwhelming force, having gathered recruits as he went. However, as the column neared Sandwich, Harold learned that Tostig had discovered he was coming and had boarded his vessels and cleared out.

Tostig's force was growing. Before pulling out of Sandwich, he had pressed into service all the able-bodied sailors he could find in that port city and had ordered them to man the royal vessels he had captured at anchor in Sandwich harbour. It turned out that there were more ships than he could find crews for, and he was forced to leave many of the vessels behind in his flight. Tostig had now been joined by his old friend and former deputy, Copsig, one of his few loyal associates who had managed to escape the wrath of the Northumbrian rebels. Copsig, still working for Tostig, had hired seventeen ships and their crews of fighting Norsemen, recruiting them from the Orkney Islands, off the north-east coast of Scotland. Altogether, Tostig's force now numbered about sixty ships, a significant force.

With the wind still at his back, Tostig sailed his fleet past the mouth of the Thames and up along England's eastern coast. He next landed on the northern coast of East Anglia, sending his men ashore to harass coastal villages and seize whatever plunder they could find, then quickly embarking again and sailing off before a land force could be assembled to combat them.

He then sailed up into the mouth of the Humber and stopped to ravage villages on the south bank. He was now in northern Mercia. Just across the wide estuary of the Humber lay Northumbria, where he was most hated.

The Aelfgarson brothers, Earl Edwin of Mercia and Earl Morkere of Northumbria, had been keeping track of Tostig and his army of marauders. Reports are likely to have gone out from London informing them, and they were doubtless receiving intelligence from their own sources along England's eastern coast, including a long string of coast guards. The brothers knew Tostig was coming their way and they were making plans to meet him.

By the time the feet of Tostig's mercenaries hit the muddy flats at the edge of the Humber River, Edwin, leading the Mercian fyrd, was dashing headlong toward the landing site, eager to drive the invaders back into the North Sea. When the invaders spread out to assault settlements along the south bank, the Mercian fighters took them by surprise and hacked them down as they fled toward their boats.

Tostig, who had stayed near the boats, quickly climbed back aboard his vessel while his mercenaries, having dropped their loot in their flight, ran for theirs. Most of Tostig's fleet managed to escape, but Edwin and the Mercian fyrdmen had decimated the raiders' numbers.

Regrouping at sea, Tostig and Copsig sailed out of the Humber estuary, rounded the cape at Spurn Head and pushed the fleet northward, aiming at the Northumbrian coastline. On their first attempt at a landing in Northumbria, they were confronted by Earl Morkere's

Northumbrian housecarls and fyrdmen, tough fighters dedicated to the defeat of Tostig, and the fleet turned back with few of Tostig's men having touched dry land. Additional attempts were repulsed by the Northumbrians, who seemed to follow the ships as they proceeded along the straight edge of the Yorkshire coast.

At that point, Tostig's mercenaries, including the Norsemen whom Copsig had recruited in the Orkneys, demanded a parley with Tostig and aboard his flagship told him that they had had enough, that the risks were too high and that they wanted him to turn back and allow them to return to easier pickings along the Channel coast, where they had already been.

Tostig refused.

That night, as the fleet rode at anchor safely off the Northumbrian coast and while Tostig and Copsig lay asleep in their vessels, the mercenaries, acting in concert, raised their sails and silently slipped away into the blackness, taking with them the impressed crews and the royal ships captured at Sandwich. At morning's light, Tostig could see that his armada, like his plan to use it to dethrone Harold, had vanished. His fleet had been reduced to twelve vessels, some of them nothing more than fishing boats. His army had diminished to the few desperate followers left aboard the twelve vessels, men who, despite all, remained loyal to him, men who evidently had nowhere else to turn.

Tostig himself had few places to which he could turn and even fewer men to turn to for help. With remarkable resilience, however, he now determined to make straight to one of them.

People who knew Tostig found it hard to understand, but the friendship between him and Malcolm III, king of Scotland, formed during the time when Tostig was earl of Northumbria, had remained steadfast over what was for Tostig many turbulent years. The story was that Tostig and Malcolm had together sworn a blood oath, drawing and mingling their blood to seal their pledge to be and remain friends and allies, closer than brothers, forever loyal to each other, come what may. Now, with his grandiose plans in tatters, it was to Malcolm, nicknamed Canmore, or Ceanmor, Gaelic for 'Big Head', son of King Duncan I and victor over Macbeth, that the angry and desperate Tostig hopefully turned.

The twelve vessels that were the remnant of his fleet weighed anchor and with the wind still behind them set sail for the land of the

Scots. The tiny fleet bore north by north-west, following the Northumbrian coastline, then turned north-westward, rounding the coast of ancient Lothian and sailing into the Firth of Forth, then proceeded westward to make a landing on the north bank of the river. After disembarking, Tostig led his remaining followers to Malcolm's palace at Dunfermline.

If Malcolm was displeased to see his old friend, he apparently managed to conceal his feelings and he eventually allowed Tostig to make his appeal. From where Malcolm stood, however, there wasn't much that could be done about King Harold. To get to Harold, Malcolm would have to march through Northumbria. There was no way, Malcolm would point out to Tostig, that Morkere and his thanes were going to let an army of Scots come through Northumbria. They would see his entry as a threat and would oppose him as soon as he crossed their border. He would have to fight every step of the way.

And after fighting his way through Northumbria, he would run head-on into Edwin's Mercian army and have to go through the same thing with them.

Tostig perhaps offered an alternative. Malcolm could take his troops by sea, circumventing Northumbria and Mercia. Malcolm had ships. Tostig had some. They could get more.

Malcolm probably responded with another dose of reality. As soon as the Northumbrians found out that he had loaded his army onto ships and put out into the North Sea, Malcolm would explain, the Northumbrians would come pouring across the border. With its army at sea, Scotland would be virtually defenceless. If Morkere himself didn't order an invasion, or even border raids, there were among his thanes some who would leap at the chance to move into Scotland.

Malcolm did allow Tostig some encouragement. He said he could provide Tostig with a base and some other support. He could also give him a suggestion: There was one man left, whom Tostig had not yet been to see, who could help him: Harald Hardrada, king of Norway.

13

THE HARD MAN
JUNE 1066

Harald Sigurdsson was fifteen years old when he first went to war and suffered his first battle wound. His side lost, and his half-brother, Olaf, the king of Norway (who later became St Olaf), for whose cause Harald fought, lost his life in that same conflict, trying to undo a rebellion that had deposed Olaf the year before. But in that fight Harald, a big, raw-boned kid at the time, well over six feet tall, discovered a couple of things about himself. One was that fighting, the thrill of the battle, was something he totally enjoyed. The other was that he was unusually good at it.

There was a term that Norsemen used to describe their warriors who, with sword or axe firmly in hand, gleefully hacked and slashed their fellow humans, enemies or merely hapless victims, in furious, bloodlustful frenzies, exhilarated by slaughter and mayhem. Such warriors were called 'berserkers'. Going into battle, they drove themselves berserk, howling like wolves or growling like bears, baring their teeth and biting their shields and foaming at the mouth and recklessly plunging into combat like mad animals, believing they were made invincible by their intense ferocity.

Harald Sigurdsson, who grew into a giant of a man, with massive hands and steely arms, deep chest and thick waist, huge head and long, flowing blond hair, became a berserker.

Following the defeat and death of Olaf at the crucial Battle of Stiklestad on 29 July 1030, young Harald, a prince of Norway who had been deserted by most of his royal retainers, fled with a single loyal follower into the refuge of Norway's dense forests. There he hid from his enemies until he recovered from his wounds. With his aide he then slipped out of Norway, crossed the Baltic Sea and entered Russia, then made his way to Novgorod, where he won the favour of Novgorod's King Jaroslav as well as the heart of Jaroslav's daughter Elizabeth. He also got himself a job in the king's army.

After a couple of years of no fighting, Harald grew restless and asked the king for permission to leave, promising Elizabeth he would return to her. With a small band of followers, navigating the river routes used by the Vikings of earlier years, he worked his way south through Russia down to the Black Sea and the ancient, storied city of Byzantium, capital of the Byzantine empire, the eastern remnant of the old Roman empire, ruled by the cunning, cruel and corrupt Empress Zoe, an ageing beauty with an eye for younger men.

Harald soon found promise of the action he craved. Zoe was planning an invasion of Sicily, which had been occupied by the fierce and hated Saracens (which was what western Europeans then called Muslims, except for the Spanish, who called them 'Moors'). Harald quickly volunteered. When he presented his credentials to Zoe's general, Harald seemed so impressive that the general, George Maniakes, put him in command of the imperial bodyguard, a unit of professional soldiers comparable to English and Scandinavian house-carls, made up mostly of tough Norse mercenaries and called the Varangian Guard.

From 1038 to 1040 Harald the berserker fought Saracens in eight major engagements in Sicily and North Africa. A nominal Christian, he made a pilgrimage to Jerusalem, slaughtering highwaymen and others who preyed on pilgrims as he went, leaving gifts at the traditional tomb of Christ and washing himself in the Jordan River.

Harald's reputation for cunning was as great as his fame as a fighter. Unable to crack the defences of a Sicilian town he had besieged, he feigned death from the illness from which he was temporarily suffering and had some of his men appeal to the priests of the town to let them give their leader a Christian funeral in one of the town's churches, a request the priests granted. The town's gate was opened, and a procession of Harald's soldiers, several of them bearing a coffin, marched slowly through the gate and into the town, the priests joining the solemn cortege. After they had passed within the walls, one of Harald's men blew a signal blast on a horn and the men carrying the coffin dropped it, and Harald's troops drew their weapons from beneath their cloaks and held the gate open so that the rest of their force could pour into the town. Harald's soldiers then butchered the men of the town, including the priests, sacked the town and took everything of value that they could carry.

On his return to Novgorod, now a man made wealthy by his years of plunder, he delightedly claimed the princess Elizabeth as his bride. He then set out for new conquests.

He went to Denmark, made an alliance with Sweyn Estrithsson, the Godwinsons' cousin who was the embattled king of Denmark, then returned to Norway, now ruled by his nephew Magnus, the son of Olaf. Magnus had been at war with Sweyn Estrithsson for years. Deciding that he didn't want to face both Sweyn and Harald, whose intimidating reputation had preceded him to his homeland, Magnus offered to buy off his Uncle Harald. He promised him a share of the Norwegian kingdom in exchange for some of Harald's treasure and Harald's joining the fight against Sweyn. Harald accepted the bribe and double-crossed Sweyn.

A few years later, in the autumn of 1047, Magnus was seriously injured in a horse-riding accident. Sensing that his end was near and wishing to put things in order before his passing, on his deathbed he bequeathed his share of the kingdom of Norway to Harald. And to Sweyn Estrithsson he gave what amounted to a quit-claim deed to the kingdom of Denmark.

Harald, however, refused to accept the Danish part of Magnus's will and after Magnus died and he became king, he determined to continue the war with Sweyn in hopes of adding Denmark to his new holdings. From then until 1064 Harald had tried to overthrow Sweyn, annually attacking the Danish coasts, ravaging city and countryside alike, hoping to crush Danish resistance.

All his attempts at taking Denmark proved in vain, however, and at last he agreed to give up the futile fight and sign a peace treaty with Sweyn who, already once betrayed by Harald, continued to keep a wary eye on him even after accepting the treaty.

During those years, while still married to Elizabeth and the father of two daughters – Maria and Ingegerd – by her, Harald had found new love. She was Thora, daughter of a Norwegian nobleman, and with little care for what the Church thought about such things, Harald married her, keeping Elizabeth as his wife as well. By Thora, Harald had two sons, Magnus and Olaf.

Also during those years, as his reputation spread, he gained a nickname that was to distinguish him from all other Harolds and Haralds in his time and throughout history. The Norwegian word 'hardrada' is translated literally into English as 'hard counsel', but its meaning was more like 'hard man' – as in 'a hard man to deal with'. Harald Sigurdsson, the berserker, the giant and powerful warrior, the terrifying and cunning chieftain, the man who was accustomed to getting what he wanted, one way or another, became known as Harald Hardrada. King Harald, the hard man.

In June 1066 King Harald Hardrada was feeling restless. His plan to take over Denmark had been thwarted, his campaign against the Danish ended. It had been two years since he'd been in a good, bloody fight, and he missed the action. He lacked a challenge and, at fifty-one years of age, he felt his life had gone empty. He had been taking out some of his frustration on his own subjects, ruling as a despot, disgruntled, harsh and stubborn.

Then into his court one day that month came someone with a proposal that sounded interesting.

Harald knew Tostig by reputation, knew of his kinship with Sweyn Estrithsson of Denmark and his connection by marriage with Count Baldwin of Flanders. He of course knew, too, that Tostig's brother Harold was the new king of England. But with his mind on things close to home lately, he hadn't kept up with Tostig's search for an ally to depose Harold.

Tostig's appeal to Hardrada's interest likely focused on Hardrada's tenuous claim to the English crown, which once had been possessed by Canute and Harthacanute and which Harthacanute had willed to King Magnus, Hardrada's predecessor. The claim was based on the premise that Magnus, not Edward, was the rightful king of England, although Magnus had chosen not to press his claim to the crown. The argument went that what was Magnus's had, through succession, become Hardrada's. Hardrada, then, should choose whether he would assert his claim to England's crown or acquiesce in its assumption by Harold Godwinson.

Actually, Hardrada had for some time been considering an attack on the eastern coast of England to assert his claim, but had never decided on it. Prodded by Tostig, he was showing new interest. Tostig undoubtedly promised Hardrada much more than he could deliver, and eventually Hardrada was won over. Tostig at last had a deal – and a powerful partner.

14

THE LONG WAIT
JULY 1066

I n July, the increasingly impatient Duke William moved out of his palace in Rouen to be closer to where the action was taking place, which was the mouth of the River Dives, about sixty-five miles west of Rouen. There, where it emptied itself into the wider waters of the bay of the Seine, the river was like a lake whose shores, lapped by relatively deep waters and sheltered from Channel storms, were well suited for the launching and harbouring of a great host of ships. It was there that the duke's invasion fleet was being assembled, many of the vessels being constructed at shipyards on the banks of the Dives, many others being finally fitted there after having been built beside rivers elsewhere in Normandy and sailed to the Dives estuary.

There also William's army was gathering, entire units and individual adventurers and fortune seekers, streaming in by horseback and on foot from Maine, Anjou, Brittany, Flanders and Scandinavia, from wherever the duke's appeal for fighting men had been heard. Towns and the countryside around the mouth of the Dives, already swollen by the numbers of shipwrights and vendors engaged in the construction of William's fleet, were beginning to overflow with armed strangers.

William foresaw problems in the sudden swelling of the area's population. He instructed his commanders to have announcements made in public places. There was to be no foraging. These soldiers of fortune and other volunteers would have to pay for their food and drink. There was to be no trespassing. Landowners must give their permission before the men could camp on their land or use their buildings. There was to be no molestation of the citizens, particularly the women. The penalty for any violation of the duke's rules, he promised, would be swiftly applied and severe. His commanders were to make sure everyone knew the rules and anyone found violating any one of them would be made an example to all other possible offenders.

Amid the shipwrights and soldiers gathered at the mouth of the Dives there was discovered an intruder who was determined by William's officers to be a spy for King Harold. The man was brought to the duke, who told him that Harold was wasting his money buying the services of spies to find out what William was up to. He told Harold's agent that he was making no secret of his plan to invade England and he said he wanted the spy to go back to Harold and deliver a message. 'Tell him', William said, 'that his fears will be over and that he will be able to live in peace to the end of his days if by the end of this year he has not seen me in the exact place where he thought he was most secure.' The duke then ordered the man released.

As soon as he was gone, William's counsellors began to voice their worry about his bravado, protesting that Harold already had enough of an advantage over them, why give him the benefit of knowing what they were doing and planning? William was unmoved by their arguments. He told them, in effect, that what Harold had to his advantage – greater numbers especially – was no match for the advantage they had, a righteous cause. Besides, he told them, numbers alone don't win wars; courage is what wins wars.

King Harold had established a headquarters on the Isle of Wight and there he was gathering a fleet that would number up to 400 vessels, including patrol boats that were scouring the northern reaches of the English Channel, looking for any sign of approaching Normans, and water-borne transports that could, with a favourable wind, quickly carry English troops to engage the invaders at any landing site opposite the coast of Normandy. Since the entire expanse of England's Channel coast lay open to Norman invaders, Harold had decided not to try to guess the exact spot at which William would land in order to station enough troops there to repel him. Instead he would keep a large, mobile force at Wight and dispatch it in answer to the summons of his coast guards when the Normans came ashore, wherever they came ashore.

Harold may well have been thinking that William was using Tostig to probe England's coastal defences. It would make sense that Tostig's hit-and-run attacks were a preliminary to a massive assault by the Norman invasion force. Harold may have thought William intended him to chase Tostig up the coast with his housecarls, leaving Wessex under-manned and allowing William to come ashore at a weak spot discovered by Tostig's assaults.

With the arrival of summer the question of when to call out the fyrd remained a critical dilemma. Harold evidently still believed that William would come between June and August, when wind and weather were favourable. Harold was expecting to sight the invasion fleet sailing toward him any day, and so it made sense to start calling out the fyrd now. The danger in that move was that William, either by design or for some other reason, would not come by the end of August. In that case, Harold would run the risk of having to fight with-out fyrdmen, since their service duty would expire after two months and if called in late June or early July, they would be back home in early September, busy with gathering in their crops and preparing for winter. If William did not come by September, England could be fac-ing an enormous disaster in October.

Harold doubtlessly felt the heavy weight of a decision regarding the fyrd. Call them now, call them later; call them too soon, call them too late. Whichever way he decided, he would be gambling. His reasoning may have gone like this: The Bastard was eager to come; in his shoes, Harold would feel the same way – do it now. Although he couldn't be sure if William would come ashore in one massive assault or in two or more, landing at one site or more than one, there was one thing Harold did feel sure about: William would come by early September. Only bad weather or God's own hand would prevent him.

At last the decision was made. They would begin calling out the fyrd, starting with the fyrdmen of Sussex, which, Harold must have fig-ured, had the likeliest landing sites.

One of Harold's next tasks was to go to Bosham and have Edith Swan's Neck and the children take precautions. The entire family was to move to Harold's estate in Oxfordshire. He would want them to realise the danger and perhaps for Edith and the older children he would spell out the perils. If William was able to secure a beachhead and push inland, they could expect him to do his worst to demoralise the people and crush their resistance. There would be mass slaughter of civilians, including women and children. No woman or girl of any age would be safe from rape or other violence. The Bastard would seize hostages and mutilate many of them; he had a history of butchery of people who resisted him. He would burn villages and farms, burn homes. England should expect a campaign of terror reaching as far as the Bastard's troops were able to penetrate. Everything was at risk for Englishmen – their lives, their homes, their families, their country, their way of life, their independence, their future and the future of English men and women yet to be born.

After he had been to Bosham, while he was back on the Isle of Wight, Harold received bad news: Tostig had found an ally in Oslo. Harald Hardrada had enlisted in his cause. Harold's sources reported that Hardrada was readying his fleet, that he had an army already formed, and Tostig and his mercenaries were part of it.

Now Harold faced two invasions, both imminent. Doubtless his strategy, unavoidably, was to meet them one at a time. Harold very probably expected Hardrada and Tostig to cross the North Sea and come ashore somewhere in Northumbria, which was where, he knew, Tostig wanted to be. He perhaps realised there was a chance they would hit Mercia first, but in either case, Hardrada and Tostig were, first of all, a matter for the Earls Edwin and Morkere primarily. Harold undoubtedly would inform the Aelfgarson brothers of Hardrada's intentions, and they presumably had their own sources of intelligence.

There was other, brighter news that came to Harold from London. Alditha, Harold's queen, was pregnant.

15
THE LAND RAVAGER
JULY 1066–SEPTEMBER 1066

In his private rooms in the royal palace in Trondheim, also known as Nidaros, the Norwegian capital on the Atlantic side of the peninsula, King Harald Hardrada, a hundred worrisome details swimming in his head, would have been in no mood to argue as he told his wife Elizabeth, the mother of his two daughters, that he wanted her and the girls to go with him.

He perhaps explained that he wanted Maria, his eldest and favourite, along with her younger sister, Ingegerd, to feel a part of a great historic event. He doubtlessly assured Elizabeth that they would not be in danger. They were to accompany him and his invasion army only as far as the Orkney Islands. The girls and Elizabeth were to stay in the Orkneys at the palace of the brothers Paul and Erlend Torfinnson, who, by Hardrada's appointment, had succeeded their late father, Torfinn, as earls of Orkney. Both were single and highly marriageable.

Elizabeth probably suspected her husband of an ulterior motive. She likely would have guessed that Harald was planning to use their nubile princess daughters as bait to lure the young earls and their force of Orkney Islanders into his invasion army. That was precisely what he intended to do, even though Maria was already engaged.

Hardrada had issued orders to conscript half of all the able-bodied young men of Norway, and his plan was to assemble that half of his

militia, the most enthusiastic of his fighting subjects, into a tough, hell-
for-leather army of berserkers who would swarm over England's
defenders and slash and smash their way to victory. Orders were for the
militiamen to make their way to Solund Island, at the mouth of the
Sogne fjord, north of Bergen, and report for duty there. Most would
come by boat, travel by water being the fastest way to get around in
Norway and reasonable enough to expect of the militiamen, since
most Norwegians were practiced sailors.

From the Sogne fjord Hardrada's invasion force would then sail to
the Shetland Islands, then to the Orkney Islands, picking up additional
recruits at each stop, then sail south to Scotland and on to join Tostig
and his force for a combined assault on the English coast and a swift
penetration inland.

By late July, King Harald Hardrada's army had begun forming. The
ambitious mobilisation and invasion plans drawn up by Hardrada and
Tostig were being realised. Hardrada himself was taking care of several
remaining last-minute details before collecting Elizabeth and their
daughters and sailing from Trondheim to assume command of the
army gathering on the shores of Solund Island.

One important thing he had to do before leaving Trondheim was to
meet with his son Magnus, now about seventeen years old, the older of
his two boys. He had appointed Magnus his co-king, which would
make the passing of the crown from his own head to Magnus's much
easier and simpler should he be killed or incapacitated – which of
course he would have told Magnus was not going to happen but for
which they naturally had to be prepared. Magnus would, in his father's
absence, rule until the king returned.

Hardrada also had to say goodbye to Thora, his other wife, the
mother of his sons, and let her know that Magnus would take care of
things for him while he was gone. If she asked about his plans for Olaf,
the younger son, he would have told her that Olaf was going with him.
And if she protested that he was only fifteen, he is likely to have
reminded her that he was fifteen when he first went to war.

The king of Norway had one last thing to do before boarding his
ship, which awaited him, along with a flotilla of escort vessels, at a
berth in the River Nid, near the Trondheim Palace.

The remains of the late King Olaf, Harald Hardrada's half-brother,
dead for thirty-six years, victim of a rebellion, lay in a vault at the cen-

tre of a shrine inside the Church of St Clement in Trondheim. Elaborately decorated with gold and silver and precious gems, the shrine was barred by a protective metal grating, the gate to which was kept locked with a padlock.

Early on the morning he was to depart from Trondheim to join his troops, King Harald Hardrada made a visit to the Church of St Clement, demanded the padlock's key in the rectory, then entered the church and made his way to the shrine of King Olaf. He unlocked the padlock, opened the metal gate and stepped inside the shrine, then slipped to his knees beside the burial vault. While his lips moved in silence, he took from its sheath on his belt a knife and moving its sharp blade across a lock of his hair, he cut off a wad of it and placed it beside the vault. Then he took the knife and trimmed off the ends of his fingernails, gathered the trimmings into a little pile and placed them next to the wad of hair.

Moments later he rose to his feet, stood staring at the vault, as if in contemplation of its contents, then slowly turned around and slipped out of the shrine's enclosure. He replaced the padlock and locked it, then tested it to make sure it was secure. Satisfied, he strode out of the church, the key still in his hand, and, collecting a small group of retainers as he stepped outside the building, he walked briskly down to the water's edge, stopped abruptly on the riverbank and pitched the padlock key far out into the River Nid.

He watched the tiny splash it made, then turned to his retainers and told them he was ready to go. Seeking supernatural help for the coming campaign, he had appealed to and sacrificed to the spirit of Olaf, the dead king, a Christian zealot who had been killed – martyred, some said – for his efforts to impose Christianity on reluctant Norwegian warriors. To make sure that no one, friend or enemy, stole into the shrine after him to reverse the good-luck spell he had cast, Harald had thrown away the key.

It must have been a sight that made Hardrada's berserker blood surge. More than 200 longships, many of them capable of carrying up to 250 men, propelled by as many as thirty-six pairs of oars or by a large, square mainsail and a jib, lay beached or rode gently at anchor in the Sogne fjord. The ships' awnings would be drawn over the waists of the ships to provide shelter for the waiting crews and passengers. Along the side rails were mounted the decorated shields of the crews, grotesque symbols of power and death, birds and beasts both real and mythical, skulls and weapons, painted on the arrayed shields in gleaming colours.

In addition, there were the ships of burden, the *byrdinger*, the transports that would carry the army's supplies. There were also smaller vessels that would bear fighting men. Altogether, it was an armada of more than 240 ships.

Hardrada likely smiled when he saw the fleet, spread into the fjord and across the banks of the craggy island, the horde of fighting men who had rowed or sailed the vessels to this spot idling aboard them or on shore, restlessly awaiting the king's arrival. He didn't know his army's numbers yet, but already he could see there were many thousands of them, armed and equipped.

At a meeting with his chief lieutenants, Hardrada gave them the news they were eager to hear. They would sail on the first favourable wind, he told the group – which included Styrkar, his chief of staff, and Eystein Orre and Nicholas Thorbergson, both brothers of his wife Thora.

On 12 August the prevailing wind began streaming out of the north-east, just what Hardrada and his horde of berserkers were waiting for. The warriors boarded their vessels, weighed anchors and, lining up in a long and fearsome parade of warships, sailed smartly out of the Sogne fjord and into the Atlantic Ocean, sails filled with the fresh breeze, all ships heading westward for the fleet's first destination, the Shetland Islands, an archipelago of some hundred islands, most of them too small to be inhabited, clustered 200 miles off Norway's west coast.

At the Shetlands, Hardrada's invasion army rested briefly, re-victualled and collected a few additional shiploads of fighting men, Hardrada's main reason for making the stop. From the Shetlands, the armada turned south-westward and made for the Orkneys, a fertile archipelago of about seventy islands, many of them uninhabited, lying about a hundred miles, port to port, from the Shetlands, and, like the Shetlands, a territory of Norway ever since Norwegian Vikings had overrun and seized the islands in the ninth century.

Upon the arrival of his fleet at Hrossey, the Orkneys' main island, King Harald would find that his young earls, Paul and Erlend Torfinnson, were awaiting him and his royal party, and the impressive fleet of warships as well, with high and happy expectations. The brothers escorted the royal visitors to Birsay, a settlement on the north-west corner of the main island, then to the Brough of Birsay, a rocky islet just offshore, where the old earl, Torfinn, who had been lord of the Orkneys for fifty years, had built a church and a castle. It was in that castle that Elizabeth and the girls would stay while Hardrada was gone.

The young princesses evidently worked Hardrada's desired effect on the young earls. They both signed on to his campaign.

The addition of Earls Paul and Erlend would make a significant difference to the campaign, Hardrada was apparently thinking. Their mother, Ingebjorg, the widow of old Torfinn, had recently remarried, and her new husband was King Malcolm of Scotland, Tostig's old friend who had refused him troops. Malcolm had granted estates in Scotland to his new wife's two sons, tying the young earls to him and the interests of the Orkneys to the interests of Scotland. Now the Orkneys, through their young earls, had declared for the Norse invasion of England and the overthrow of Harold Godwinson. Malcolm would have to take notice.

The Torfinnson brothers allowed the Orkneys to become a gathering place for assorted potential allies of Hardrada – Norse descendants and sympathisers from various parts of the British Isles and elsewhere in the north, men who would prefer to have a Norwegian king rule England rather than a Saxon. And Hardrada was able to recruit not only Shetlanders and men of the Orkneys but fighting men from the Faroe Islands far to the north of Scotland, from Iceland, from the islands off western Scotland, from the islands off Ireland and from northern Scotland itself, men who included an Irish king and an Icelandic prince, all banding together in a Viking-like Nordic alliance against the Anglo-Saxons and their king, Harold Godwinson.

At the end of August Hardrada's army, markedly increased by the recruits gained in the Orkneys, was ready to sail again. The wind was still favourable, coming steadily out of the north-east. Hardrada's adventurers rowed their vessels out into Scapa Flow, then turned southward, drawing in their oars and raising their sails to catch the breeze, heading for Scotland, the last stop before their appointed rendezvous with Tostig and the army of mercenaries he had managed to put together.

News of Hardrada's approach, long noticed as the armada made its way down Scotland's east coast, had already reached the settlements along the Firth of Forth, and fighting men disposed to Hardrada's cause were already gathering along the banks of the firth as the fleet of long-boats and accompanying vessels sailed westward along the firth's north shore, then anchored at the mouth of the Forth, off from Dunfermline.

While his lieutenants enlisted volunteers along the waterfront, Hardrada, perhaps taking the Earls Paul and Erlend with him, paid a visit to King Malcolm in the royal castle at Dunfermline. He would point out to Malcolm that the Orkney earls had thrown in with him and he would make an appeal for Malcolm to do the same. Malcolm, however, probably told Hardrada that nothing about his situation had changed since he had talked with Tostig. He simply couldn't afford to risk leaving Scotland open to hostiles in Northumbria. He couldn't afford to risk being on the losing side of a war against the king of England either, but he probably didn't mention that. Malcolm was probably thinking that if he joined Hardrada, he had little to gain if Hardrada won his war with King Harold, but he had everything to lose, including his life, if Hardrada lost it. Malcolm was determined to sit this one out.

By the first week of September, Hardrada was gone from Dunfermline. His armada rowed out of the Firth of Forth, turned south-eastward and set sail for the mouth of the River Tyne, where Tostig's force, now assembling aboard their vessels in the North Sea off the Yorkshire coast, would merge with Hardrada's army and the con-spirators' campaign to capture England and its crown would begin.

Tynemouth was the tiny fishing village that stood where the River Tyne met the North Sea. At the outskirts of the village, to the west, lay the rocky ruins of the eastern end of a remarkable wall that once had spanned the country, from the Irish Sea to the North Sea. The Roman emperor Hadrian had ordered it built to keep invaders out of Britain nine centuries earlier. Now, east of Tynemouth, offshore in the North Sea waters, Hardrada and Tostig were about to join forces for a new invasion of the land that Emperor Hadrian had vainly sought to protect.

On the morning of 7 September the new invaders came crashing upon the unprotected English coast. They ran their ships ashore between the estuaries of the rivers Tees and Esk, in the north-east cor-ner of Northumbria, and burst from them howling and screaming, thousands of berserkers simultaneously leaping overboard, splashing through knee-deep water and charging upon the shore, brandishing swords and axes.

At the centre of the first rank of shouting warriors, Hardrada's standard bearer came running, his hands gripping the long wooden staff from which flapped King Harald's own battle flag, feared from the North Sea to the Mediterranean. It had a stark white background, and at its centre was a large, glossy-black raven, the predaceous, omnivorous bird of Nordic myth, the *Landeyda* – the Land Ravager.

Easily overwhelming the sparsely settled coastal area, Hardrada and Tostig's armies spread into the Northumbrian countryside, burning towns and farms, plundering and butchering their inhabitants without serious opposition. Emboldened, they returned to their ships and sailed farther south, to Scarborough, another fishing town.

When Hardrada drew his ships up onto the sandy beach and dispatched a detail to demand that the officials of the town surrender it to him, they refused and when he then ordered a unit of his soldiers to take the town, the townspeople barricaded themselves in their houses and repulsed Hardrada's troops. Not one to spend his men needlessly, Hardrada then led a group of soldiers to the top of the cliff that overlooked the town and had his men build a fire on the edge of the height. When the pile of wood was blazing, he ordered his men to pull out the flaming logs and branches and hurl them down onto the roofs below. After most of the houses in town had caught fire, the townspeople surrendered. Hardrada slaughtered every last one of them and burned Scarborough to the ground.

From Scarborough, one part of Hardrada's army marched farther down the coast, the remainder of the force keeping up with them by sea, passing along the shore of Filey Bay as they continued along the coastline. Near the shore of Bridlington Bay the invasion force encountered a unit of Northumbrian fyrdmen who had formed a defensive line to block the invaders' path. With enormously superior numbers, Hardrada's troops overwhelmed the Northumbrians and put them all to the sword.

Hardrada and Tostig now decided to abandon the coast and move directly to their first major objective: the city of York, capital of Northumbria. York had been the centre of the rebellion against Tostig, the place where his troubles had begun. In his view, it was the city that his enemies had stolen from him. It was the place that symbolised the office, the power, the prestige, the dignity and the wealth that had been taken from him. He was burning to take it all back.

York lay inland, about thirty-five miles south-west of Scarborough, but it was reachable by water as well as land. Given the choice, Hardrada, with a Viking's heart, picked the water route, with good reasons. His ships would serve as his base; they were an extension of his territory, his home ground. They would give him more speed and mobility as well. And with wintry weather not many weeks away, his ships would soon need shelter from the sea anyway.

Going to York by water meant that the Norse troops would re-embark and the fleet would sail south-eastward once more along the English coast, down to and around Spurn Head cape and into the wide estuary of the River Humber. At the mouth of the Humber the invaders would strike their sails, man their oars and row up the river to its tributary, the River Ouse, then up the tortuous Ouse to York, altogether about seventy-five miles of rowing. Then they would disembark and assemble for the assault on York.

After two days of rowing, the fleet anchored on the right bank of the Ouse near Selby. By that point, the only significant occurrence had been the fleet's lead vessels spotting Northumbrian ships upriver at one long straight stretch of the Ouse. At the sight of the miles-long line of Norse longboats, however, the Northumbrian vessels had quickly turned around and retreated upstream.

After a night's rest, Hardrada's fleet rowed to the village of Riccall, which lay east of the river, about fifteen miles below York by water, about twelve by land. There they landed again, with hours of daylight left. The river was severely narrowing, which had become a worry to Hardrada. He feared that the diminishing manoeuvrability of his ships in constricted waters might make it easy for the English to lay a trap for him. He was also wary of the Northumbrian ships that had been sighted earlier. He had learned from informants that the Northumbrians had rowed from the Ouse up into the River Wharfe and were lying near Tadcaster, about twelve land miles south-west of York. So he decided to leave his longboats along the banks of the Ouse, about a mile below the spot where the Wharfe flowed into it, and establish a base to guard his rear from a possible attack by the Northumbrian vessels. From that base he would march to York.

Two roads led from Riccall to York, one following the winding course of the Ouse, the other more of a straight line to the north. The two roads converged at Gate Fulford, a village about two miles south of

York. To mass his troops on York as swiftly as possible, Hardrada ordered them up both roads, sending two halves of the army streaming northward simultaneously, filling the roadways with the terrifying sight and sounds of thousands of marching soldiers, foreign soldiers. Farmers and villagers would run with their families from their homes, hastily fleeing the columns of marchers, running for their lives.

At Gate Fulford the merged roadways, now one, ran parallel to the Ouse on a raised causeway, several hundred yards east of the river. On the east side of the causeway there was a water-filled ditch, apparently created to provide fill for the causeway, and farther east, beyond the ditch, lay a broad, watery fen. From the edges of the roadway the ground sloped gently down on either side, toward the river on the west and the ditch on the east.

Early in the day on Wednesday 20 September, Hardrada and Tostig, at the head of their invasion army, stood at the south end of that raised roadway, staring toward York, its spires within their sight. They watched while, near the roadway's opposite end, an army deployed to block their advance and defend the city of York, the defenders moving steadily forward and extending their front from the roadway to the river as they advanced.

It had been two weeks since the Norsemen had first swarmed ashore on the Northumbrian coast, and reports of their marauding and their movement had been flowing daily into Earl Morkere's palace in York. Within hours of receiving the reports from Scarborough, Morkere had called out the Northumbrian fyrd, had marshalled his housecarls and had summoned help from his brother, Earl Edwin of Mercia, who had quickly responded with Mercian housecarls and fyrdmen. The defenders had assembled at York and were now ready to face their old enemy, Tostig, and the army of invaders led by the new foe, Harald Hardrada.

Hardrada and Tostig immediately prepared to confront the advancing defenders. Hardrada moved off the roadway and toward the river to extend his army's front westward all the way to the river's edge and to command the army's left. Tostig held the roadway, commanding the invaders' right front, which ended a few yards away at the water-filled ditch.

With Hardrada went his brother-in-law, Eystein Orre, commanding a section of the invaders' line. Eystein's brother, Nicholas, commanded another. The Orkney earls, Paul and Erlend, were placed by Hardrada

in positions behind the lines that would expose them to no more haz-
ard than necessary. Hardrada's young son, Olaf, had been left to help
guard his father's fleet at Riccall, a job that effectively removed him
from harm's way.

On the English right front, opposing Hardrada's command, the
defenders were commanded by Edwin. Morkere commanded on the
English left, facing Tostig's command. Morkere's troops, now advancing
on the run, coming straight down the roadway and along its shoulders,
hit the Norsemen's line first. They did so with such force that the
invaders' right flank was bent backward and soon was in danger of
being turned, though the Norsemen were bloodying the English as
they pushed and hacked their way into the line of invaders. With no
room to manoeuvre, the Norsemen kept giving ground, but slowly.

From his position near the river, where the bulk of both armies were
engaging across the extent of the grassy flat between the river and the
roadway, Hardrada, probably the tallest man on the field of battle, could
see his right flank being pressed backward. He watched as the centre of
the English line began tending toward its left, gradually shifting toward
the spot of less resistance, weakening its centre as it strengthened its left.

Hardrada ordered his trumpeter to sound the charge. Responding
instantly, the shrieking, screaming, howling berserkers burst forward,
weapons flailing, and slashed their way through the centre of the
defenders' line while Hardrada and his units, with the Land Ravager
standard bearer running in front of the king, crashed against the
English right.

The defenders' line broke in the centre, and their entire left front
was cut off, Eystein Orre's command now behind it and at its right
flank, and Tostig's stubborn troops in its face. The Norsemen devastated
the English line, continuing to assault it from its centre, then across the
roadway, to the water-filled ditch, across which scores of Englishmen
were desperately fleeing as their ranks disintegrated. One report, from
a Norseman, said the ditch and the nearby fen were so covered with
the corpses of the fallen defenders that a man could cross both ditch
and fen without getting his feet wet.

On the river side of the line, the defenders were no more fortunate.
Hardrada's troops, driven by their chief berserker, shattered the English
line, driving it back toward York and west into the River Ouse. Those
caught fleeing into the river were overtaken and slaughtered, the Ouse

at one point turning red with blood, the current carrying off many dozens of English corpses.

The Battle of Gate Fulford had turned into a debacle. The generals of the defenders' army, the Earls Morkere and Edwin, seeing the disaster, escaped the battle and disappeared. The bloody remnant of their shredded army either retreated in disarray into York or vanished as individuals into the countryside, their flight leaving the field entirely to Hardrada and Tostig and the cheering, shouting, maddened army of Norse invaders.

The dead and dying were everywhere. The Norsemen had suffered severe casualties, but nothing compared to the losses of the English. The fyrds of Northumbria and Mercia had been annihilated. Those few fyrdmen who had survived no longer constituted a fighting force. Edwin and Morkere's units of housecarls had been likewise devastated. Their armies smashed, Northumbria and Mercia no longer had the means to resist the invaders. Hardrada and Tostig's victory at Gate Fulford was both huge and decisive.

Hardrada now divided his army. He ordered a large part of it, commanded by Eystein and Nicholas, to return to Riccall and the ships, there to rest, to care for the wounded and deliver news of the victory to Prince Olaf who, Hardrada knew, would be anxious to hear word from his father.

The remainder of his troops he marched to the walls of York, then left them camped just outside the city and took his bodyguard with him into the city. His plan, and Tostig's, was to capture York, to possess it for themselves, not to destroy it. Tostig, with several Northumbrian thanes who that day had deserted Morkere and joined their victorious former earl, followed eagerly along behind Hardrada.

Hardrada found that York's officials, who had viewed the massacre from a safe distance, were altogether co-operative. They agreed to everything. They would turn over the city to Hardrada, they would acknowledge him as their king and pledge him fealty, they would support him in his campaign to displace King Harold and they would give him hostages to secure the promises they were making to him.

Tostig now stepped forward and handed them a list. It was the names of people he wanted turned over to him as hostages. They were the children of the city's most prominent citizens, all of them Tostig's enemies – 150 children and young people.

The officials of York had little choice. The hostages would be rounded up, from their houses in the city and from wherever else they had taken refuge from the invaders, and delivered to Tostig.

Then Tostig decided 150 wasn't enough. He drew up a new list, this one raising the number of hostages to 500. He gave it to the members of the Northumbrian witan who had remained in York. The additional 350 hostages were to come not from York but from other parts of Northumbria. Hardrada and Tostig set a deadline for the surrender of the entire group of hostages. It was Monday 25 September, five days away.

They also agreed to a place where the hostages would be handed over, a village about six miles east of York, a location both sides decided was more tranquil and much better than York. The city's officials wanted to avoid the presence of armed Norse troops in York, and Hardrada wanted to avoid the problem of controlling his berserkers if he brought them into the city, his promise to protect York having been part of the bargain with the city fathers.

The hostage arrangements were settled then – the number, the who, the time and the place. Everything was agreed. Hardrada and Tostig, expansive after their outstanding success, then withdrew with their troops and returned to their base at Riccall to wait and to celebrate.

16

THE STAMFORD BRIDGE
SEPTEMBER 1066

On Friday 8 September, the feast day of the Nativity of St Mary, few of those Englishmen who knew what the arrival of autumn weather would do to the English Channel still believed that Duke William would come before the end of the year.

Even King Harold, at his command post on the Isle of Wight, was perhaps beginning to have doubts. Because he was once a sailor himself, he knew there was good reason to accept the seafaring wisdom of his advisors, which said that after early September, serious sailing was ended until spring. The adverse winds and seas of autumn and winter were simply too much for any but the most skilled sailors, the stoutest ships and the shortest voyages.

Another thought likely to be in the minds of Harold and his advisors was whether the fyrd should be released now. Most of the fyrdmen had already stayed past their service time. They had exhausted their own supplies, and Harold lacked enough to feed them from the provisions for his housecarls. The fleet's crews would be going home that very day, their agreement being that they would stand by until St Mary's Nativity. After that, it had been generally agreed, they would not be needed, the weather now being the nation's first defence.

By the same wisdom, Harold no longer needed to garrison the fyrd, which he lacked the means to keep on duty anyway. He finally made the decision to let the fyrdmen go home. From the moment the men were notified, England's militia army was officially disbanded. If he had to do it over again, Harold would probably not have called out the fyrd when he did, but instead would have waited another two to four weeks.

By now he was likely to have grown weary of trying to guess what William was doing. He would also have grown more frustrated by the lack of activity. By the second week of September he was probably eager to return to London, where he could find some sort of activity to occupy him. On 13 September, a Wednesday, he mounted his horse and rode off with his bodyguard.

The news from Northumbria reached London before Harold did. He received the report immediately upon his arrival in Westminster on the afternoon of Thursday 14 September. King Harald Hardrada and his army of adventurers, with Tostig at his elbow, had stormed ashore between the Tees and the Esk on 7 September, had later landed at Scarborough and burned the town, and from there had begun a march southward down the Northumbrian coast, virtually unopposed.

Harold had realised that simultaneous invasions at opposite ends of the country were possible. While the fyrd was stationed on the Channel coast, however, he had felt confident that he had enough manpower to fight two enemies at once. But with the fyrd disbanded, facing two foes simultaneously at two opposite ends of the country had become a dreadful prospect.

Harold summoned Gyrth and Leofwine and ordered the housecarls to stand ready to move out on short notice. When his brothers arrived, he told them what he planned to do. He was recalling the fyrdmen of Wessex and having them muster immediately. He felt he knew these men best of all his subjects. They were doggedly loyal to him. Most would do whatever was necessary to reprovision themselves and give the extra effort required. He would mass them with the combined housecarl forces and together march them swiftly from London to confront Hardrada and Tostig.

What Harold evidently wanted was overwhelming strength, enough to make the confrontation with the Norsemen a one-punch fight. If William were to come while the Channel coast was unmanned, Harold was probably thinking that he would be able to dispose of Hardrada and Tostig so quickly that he could immediately shift his army back to the south. Confronting William immediately after taking on Hardrada and Tostig was not the way anyone would choose to fight the Bastard. It was simply making the best of a bad turn of events.

Three days later, on Monday 18 September, King Harold, commanding his hastily reassembled army, rode out of London to confront the Norse berserkers and his own treasonous brother. Behind Harold and his bodyguard were arranged seven divisions of fighting men, streaming north toward York on the road built by the Roman conquerors of Britain some eight centuries earlier.

York lay nearly 200 miles away. Marching by day and into the night, stopping only for rest breaks, Harold's army could reach it in a week or less. Speed was essential, not just to confront Hardrada and Tostig as soon as possible but to rush back to the unprotected Channel coast as soon as possible in case Duke William should come after all.

As they marched, many on horseback, most on foot, Harold's numbers were swelled by volunteers who joined them on the way, responding to troop commanders who were making urgent appeals for recruits as they marched through the towns of England's eastern shires, through the earldoms of Leofwine, Gyrth and Waltheolf, then into the southeastern shires of Mercia.

By the sixth day of the march, Saturday 23 September, Harold's army had crossed into Northumbria and was encountering fleeing Mercian survivors of the battle at Gate Fulford. They described for Harold and his commanders the catastrophe of just three days earlier. Many of them, eager for another chance with the Norsemen who had butchered their comrades and who might soon be threatening Mercia, fell into the line of Harold's steadily advancing army, now stirred by the news of their countrymen's awful defeat.

To Harold it was news both good and bad. The Northumbrian and Mercian fighters had remained loyal to the English king and had not thrown in with Hardrada. But they had paid for their loyalty with their lives.

Harold and his army crossed the River Don and continued northwest, fording the River Aire, then heading due north for several miles before turning north-east, following the York highway to Tadcaster, which lay beside the River Wharfe, about ten miles upstream of Riccall. Harold reached Tadcaster late in the morning of Sunday 24 September and there he halted the column and ordered his army into battle formation.

York was now just nine miles away, to the north-east. Intelligence gathered from refugees in the area had informed Harold that York's officials had already surrendered the city but it had not been occupied by the Norsemen, who were waiting in their ships near Riccall. Unable to know whether Hardrada and Tostig were aware of his army's presence, Harold now ordered his commanders to assume they would fall under attack by the Norsemen as they advanced on York. If Hardrada's army was going to engage them, this would be the time, this would be the place.

Surprisingly, unaccountably, the road to York was empty, the fields and pastures on either side as serene as on any ordinary autumn day. There was no sign of an enemy anywhere, not even a sentry.

King Harold rode through York's main gate as he had done six months earlier, when he had come to York for his wedding to Lady Alditha. This time, his reception by the city fathers was doubtlessly even more enthusiastic.

Harold ordered the city's gates closed and secured once the last of his troops were inside. His intention was to block all exits from the city. Absolutely no one was to be allowed to leave. He wanted no word of his army's presence leaking out to Hardrada and Tostig.

York's mayor would explain to Harold and his chief lieutenants that Tostig and Hardrada had demanded 500 hostages and that the hostages were to be turned over to the invaders the next day. He probably also told Harold that neither Morkere nor Edwin had been seen or heard from since the battle outside Gate Fulford four days earlier.

When Harold was told that the hostages were to be turned over at Stamford Bridge, he may have asked where that was. The answer was that it was a community about six miles east of York, where the York highway and the north-south road to Market Weighton both crossed the River Derwent. At that spot there was an old bridge.

The location was fortunate, Harold would have realised. He may have been thinking that it was the first bit of good luck he had had so far – that and the fact that his arrival in York had been incredibly timely. Another day and the hostages would have been in the hands of Hardrada and Tostig.

Now supplied with the information he needed, Harold called his commanders together to lay out the plan of battle.

The sun rose bright and warm on Monday 25 September, quickly dissipating the morning's autumn crispness. The day promised to be unseasonably warm. Along the banks of the River Ouse at Riccall the Norsemen were assembling after another night of celebration and several hours of sleep under the awnings of their vessels. Breakfast was over, and the warriors were preparing for the twelve-mile march to Stamford Bridge, where they would take charge of the 500 hostages to be delivered to them by the English. An air of celebration still ran through the encampment, which extended several hundred yards along the north side of the river, allowing space enough for the 300-odd ships of Hardrada and Tostig's fleet. The men were shouting raucously to one another, joking and laughing.

When it came time to put on their equipment and fall in for the march, they found that they were uncomfortably hot in their byrnies, the knee-length leather coats studded with iron knobs and rings that they wore as armour. Most soon decided they didn't need their byrnies, so took them off and put them back in their lockers aboard their ships. Except for Tostig, the commanders didn't object, since many of them had already removed their own armour.

The Norsemen ignored Tostig. The march was too long and the sun too hot for unnecessary encumbrances. Hardrada felt as carefree as the men. He discarded his own mail coat and decided to leave about a third of his force, about 3,000 men, at Riccall. There was no point in taking everyone. They wouldn't be needed. Prince Olaf would again stay with the ships, as would Tostig's teenage sons, Skule and Ketel, as well as the young Orkney earls, the brothers Paul and Erlend. Also staying behind would be Eystein Orre, Hardrada's brother-in-law. Olaf would be in nominal charge of the camp, but his Uncle Eystein would actually command.

The order of march was casual, the column loose and long. Those who hadn't left their byrnies aboard their ships began to sweat in them as the sun rose higher in the clear sky. At the head of the invaders' column Hardrada and Tostig rode on captured English horses. Familiar with this part of the country, Tostig led the marchers on the shortest route from Riccall to Stamford Bridge, over rough roadways and cross country, passing several miles to the south and to the east of York. The column crossed the River Derwent near Kexby, about three miles south-west of Stamford Bridge, and proceeded northward on the east side of the river. It reached Stamford Bridge, on its left, about mid-morning.

The bridge carried the York to Bridlington east-west highway across the Derwent, which at this point in its sluggish course flowed from north to south through a valley about 500 yards wide. Originally built by the Romans, the bridge was constructed of wood and stone, the oaken planks of its floor nailed to beams fastened atop stone piers. Its span was about seventy feet, its width about twelve feet. Beneath it, the river, much narrower here than at the fordable shallows farther downstream, was about sixty feet across.

As they approached the village beside the bridge, the invaders would have noticed it was deserted. There was no sign of the hostages or, probably, of any other human life. Hardrada was likely then to have issued an order for the men to fall out, which, after the long, hot march, they were undoubtedly eager to do. They would scatter themselves and relax in the sun while awaiting the arrival of the hostages.

The Norse warriors who had crossed to the west side of the river would probably have been the first to hear the noise and would have looked up to see a cloud of dust above the roadway on the far side of the rise between the river on the east and the village of Gate Helmsley and the city of York on the west.

Now the games and dozing would end as the Norsemen looked up. There, on the brow of the rise, they would see wide ranks of riders and foot soldiers forming, one behind the other, stretching across the roadway far to the south and to the north, tracing the line of the western horizon.

It was immediately obvious this was not the party of hostages and compliant Northumbrian officials. The front rank was mounted, the riders' armour and weapons reflecting flashes of the bright, late-morning sun into the Norsemen's surprised eyes. As the invaders stood watching, the ranks on the rise lengthened and swelled. This was a large and formidable army the Norsemen were suddenly facing.

Perhaps now Tostig realised what it was he was seeing: Harold and his English army. Harold was not, as Tostig perhaps had guessed he would be, on the Channel coast awaiting William. He was here at Stamford Bridge, arraying his army some 400 yards away.

Tostig's first thought, as the Norse warriors on the west side of the river ran pell-mell for the bridge, apparently was to withdraw in haste to the boats at Riccall and there to collect their armour and join the troops that had been left there.

Hardrada rejected that idea. There was no time to retreat. Harold's mounted troops would overtake them and cut them down before the invaders could reach Riccall. They would have to stand here and fight. They would also immediately dispatch riders to race to the boats and tell Eystein Orre to quickly come to reinforce them.

King Harold's mounted warriors, racing to pick off the Norsemen fleeing for the east side of the river, were swiftly followed by waves of shouting fighters on foot, running across a broad front toward the river. The Norsemen, seeing that they would never make it across the river now, turned to face the Englishmen, shouting commands to form a defensive battle formation some fifty yards from the river. The English foot soldiers charged into the Norsemen's wall of resistance, slashing and axing the invaders, most of whom had been caught in the open with neither armour nor shields. They gave ground only stubbornly as Harold's Wessex fyrdmen swarmed over them with vastly superior numbers, cutting them down like wheat stalks, until the resistance on the west side of the river was all but wiped out. Bloody, bare-chested, armourless bodies were left strewn down the wide slope of the west bank, all the way from near the rise to the river.

At the water's edge the left side of the Englishmen's lines was forced to halt its headlong dash and funnel itself onto the bridge, the river being unfordable here. They soon encountered a dangerous bottle-neck. A huge, armoured berserker, with his battleaxe and his massive body, was blocking entry onto the bridge. He stubbornly withstood assaults by the Englishmen, who had little room to manoeuvre around him. He hewed them down, wildly hacking and slashing till the bodies of fallen fyrdmen themselves raised a barrier to the bridge. Forty English fighters, according to one report, were killed trying to force their way past the powerful berserker in their attempt to clear the bridge for the bottlenecked left front of the English army.

Then one fyrdman came dragging a wooden tub to the edge of the river, upstream of the bridge. He launched the tub into the current and climbed aboard, grasping his spear in one hand and the rim of the tub in the other. When the tub drifted underneath the bridge, he manoeu-vred it with his spear to a spot directly beneath the berserker. He then shoved the point of his spear up through the chink between the planks of the bridge floor and, thrusting the spear straight upward with a mighty heave, he skewered the Norseman from crotch to thorax.

The English soldiers then quickly cleared the bridge, carrying off the dead and wounded and then instantly pouring across the Stamford Bridge like water through a funnel, footmen and riders alike, dashing toward the main body of the invaders' army, which was shaping itself into battle formation about 300 yards east of the river.

Several hundred yards downstream of the bridge, the right flank of King Harold's army, riders in the first ranks, footmen behind them, was charging uncontested across the stony shallows of the Derwent, splashing through reeds at the river's edge, then into the wide, knee-deep stream and swiftly crossing to the far side with weapons and shields held high, then drawing up on the east bank to await the advance of the army's centre and left flank.

When the two parts of his army had linked up, the centre and left side having crossed the Stamford Bridge, the right side having forded the stream, Harold rode to the centre of his lines and watched as the Norsemen began forming into a large, thick, circular shield wall. He could see inside the circle a large man in an elaborate helmet astride a black horse, which he was trying to turn. Suddenly, as Harold and a group of his commanders watched, the man in the fancy helmet fell from the horse's back and landed on his buttocks on the ground.

Harold, according to the account by Snorri Sturluson, asked the men near him if they knew who the big oaf was. It was Hardrada, one of them answered. 'I think we've seen an omen', Harold responded.

The English lines now started moving forward again. When the first rank was within a hundred yards of the Norsemen's shield wall, Harold halted his army. Then he called for a contingent of his bodyguard, who immediately rode up beside him, and together, with Harold in the lead, they rode out in front of the army and halted within shouting distance of the invaders' line.

'Is Lord Tostig in this army?' Harold shouted as he reined in his horse, lifted himself from his saddle and stood in his stirrups.

A few moments passed, then Tostig, riding up to the section of the Norsemen's line closest to Harold and his party, shouted, 'Yes, I'm here.'

'Your brother King Harold sends you greetings,' Harold shouted back across the distance. 'He also sends you a message. He will give you all of Northumbria rather than have you fight him. He offers you a third of his kingdom to make peace with you.'

Tostig shouted back, 'That's a far different offer than the one of humiliation and scorn he made to me last winter! If he had made this offer then, we would not be standing here today, and many a man who is now dead would still be alive and England would be much better off now!'

Harold didn't reply.

'Tell me,' Tostig shouted again, 'if I accept King Harold's offer, what will my brother offer King Harald Sigurdsson for his efforts?'

Harold shouted back in a loud voice, 'He will give him six feet of English soil. Or perhaps a bit more since he's so big.' Six feet in which to bury him.

Tostig shouted back his answer. 'Then go and tell King Harold to get ready for battle. I've not come this far to desert my friend. We've come to fight. And we shall either take England by victory here or die in defeat.'

Harold then would tug his mount's reins, turn the horse about and, with the guards beside him and behind him, gallop back to the English lines.

Hardrada had stood listening to the exchange between Tostig and the rider who spoke, but he hadn't understood all that was said. Now as the Englishmen rode back toward their lines, again according to Snorri Sturluson, Hardrada asked Tostig, 'Who was that man who spoke?'

'That was King Harold,' Tostig told him.

'Well, why didn't you say so? I wouldn't have let him get back to his lines alive.'

'I know,' Tostig said. 'That's why I didn't tell you. Telling you would have made me his killer. I'd rather he be my killer than I his.'

Hardrada turned away from Tostig and spoke to the men who were standing nearby. 'The king of the English is a little man, but he looks good when he stands in his stirrups.' He laughed.

The offer from Harold to Tostig was evidently genuine. It sprang from the new realities of Harold's situation, and of England's. Edwin and Morkere were of no further use to him or to the country. Their armies had been smashed and they themselves had either deserted or been killed, though their bodies had not been found. The ability of Northumbrian thanes and other leading citizens to protest Tostig's restoration was gone, as was the validity of whatever argument they could make against him. Whatever else an earl might do for his people, it was nothing if he couldn't defend them against enemies. Morkere, even with assistance from his brother, had failed the first requirement of his office. Harold had never particularly cared for either of the Aelfgarson brothers and now, in his mind at least, he had dismissed them from their offices and their holdings, since they had catastrophically failed in their duty to him.

What was more, Harold knew he still must face Duke William and the Normans. He didn't want needless loss of life now at Stamford Bridge and a diminished army returning to the Channel coast. If he could trade his way to peace with Tostig, he and England and a great many of England's finest men would be the better for it. A deal with Tostig could save many lives, including the life of the country. Besides all that, Tostig was still his brother.

But, right or wrong, practical or not, Harold felt no spirit of compromise for Hardrada, whom Harold blamed for the harm thus far inflicted on Northumbria. And Tostig, whom he was willing to pardon, had turned him down. There was now no alternative to a bloody, decisive battle.

Upon reaching the English lines, Harold immediately issued the command to launch the assault. On a signal from the trumpeter, the first wave of mounted housecarls moved out swiftly, gaining speed as they plunged forward, shields before them, lances gripped in their hands, their horses thundering toward the invaders' shield wall. Thirty to forty yards from the enemy line, the riders hurled their lances into the Norsemen's formation, then turned their mounts and sped back toward their own line. They were quickly followed by second and third waves of riders who flung their lances into the clustered Norse troops, then wheeled and raced back toward the lines of English foot soldiers, now beginning to advance on a broad front. The riders dismounted then and joined the ranks of the foot soldiers, armed with swords or axes, helmeted and armoured in byrnies or hauberks, the shields of the Wessexmen painted with the fearsome dragon of Wessex, all of them jogging now at a steady pace, advancing rapidly behind the flapping standards bearing the dragon of Wessex.

Then the distance was closed and with roars of shouting the Englishmen struck the invaders' lines, the air quickly filling with yells and screams and the ringing sound of clashing metal. The battle smell was the mingled odours of sweat and vomit and excrement.

Outnumbered almost two to one, the ferocious Norse fighters managed to stubbornly hold their ground, taking severe losses but withstanding the waves of Englishmen who pressed continually against their shield wall. Under the unceasing assault, however, the immense, rough circle of the invaders' formation was, from its centre westward toward the river and eastward up the gently sloping plain, constricting ever so gradually as the English onslaught hewed gaps in the front ranks of the human wall.

As the battle passed into the afternoon it seemed at one point that the English attack had relented along one section of the Norse shield wall, and one part of the invaders' line started to move forward as if to counterattack. Hardrada commanded his berserkers to stand steady, not to separate the shield wall.

But it was too late. The briefly attenuated section of the Norse line was almost instantly penetrated by the pressing English attackers and the sally of berserkers was quickly cut off and overwhelmed.

Hardrada would shout from the centre of the circular shield wall where he was standing at the head of his reserves. He raised his axe over his head then and with his reserves behind him, ran wildly toward the breach. Rushing up beside him to fling himself into the fray with his king, young Fridrek, Hardrada's standard bearer, came with the Land Ravager emblem.

Wildly, recklessly wielding his battleaxe in both hands, Hardrada slashed into the Englishmen who were first through the shield wall's gap. Completely berserk, he cut a wide swath through the English, while his reserves hastened behind him to restore the ruptured Norse line. Then suddenly the huge old warrior's arms dropped and for an instant he stood stiffly before his head fell and his body crumpled and blood gushed from his mouth and neck and his throat gaped wide with a horrible and fatal axe wound.

Hardrada, the old berserker, was dead.

King Harold, mounted on his horse behind the English lines, saw the berserk giant go down. He ordered the trumpeter to signal a halt in the fighting, and after several minutes the Englishmen broke off and moved back from the shield wall while the Norsemen, stunned by the death of their king, held their positions. Now Harold, again with his bodyguard, rode toward the Norse line under a flag of truce. He again halted within shouting distance. Then in a loud voice he called out for Tostig.

The silence over the battlefield was eerily palpable. The time was now about three o'clock. The fighting, the butchery, had been going on, unabated till now, for more than three hours. The sun was still blazing. The dead, Norse and English alike, were lying where they had fallen. The wounded of both sides were being cared for by their comrades as best they could, the English better than the hard-pressed Norsemen. Now the heavy silence was broken by Tostig's voice.

From inside the shield wall, he shouted a request for Harold to state what was on his mind.

Harold shouted back that Tostig had now lost his friend and no longer owed him anything. He urged Tostig to lay down his arms and save his own life as well as the lives of the men who fought for him. He promised them mercy and pardon.

When Tostig asked if he still offered a third of the kingdom, Harold answered that he offered the mercy and protection of the kingdom.

Tostig responded that Harold had offered more than that earlier. Harold told him that he had rejected him then. Tostig shouted back that he rejected Harold still, that he wanted victory not charity.

Harold turned and spurred his horse and with his escort rode hurriedly back to his lines.

The battle resumed, the carnage continuing throughout the afternoon, the fierceness, vigour and determination of the Norsemen seeming inexhaustible, despite unrelenting pressure by the English upon their lines. Both sides were taking enormous losses. Then very late in the afternoon, a determined surge by a unit of housecarls and fyrdmen burst through a section of the invaders' wall and Tostig, standing beside the Land Ravager emblem, planted just inside that section of the Norse line, was caught by surprise and struck down and killed by a swarm of attackers.

While on the forward side of the circular shield wall the English were shouting over the death of Tostig, Norse cheers went up from the rear of the circle, toward the south. Eystein Orre and the 3,000 invaders who had been left behind at Riccall had finally arrived to reinforce their beleaguered comrades. The men now arriving for battle had double-timed the twelve miles from Riccall, in armour and under the hot sun, and many of them came onto the field too exhausted to raise their weapons. Many others, according to one report, fell dead without a blow having been struck, victims of heat exhaustion. Those who had managed to endure the hurried march, however, having worked themselves into berserkers' frenzy as they neared the scene of battle, now rushed to the front and flanks of the circle to throw themselves into the faces of the Englishmen. Many of them stripped off their armour to free themselves of encumbrance, wildly wielding sword and axe, careless of the sharp English metal opposing them.

The reinforcements made little difference. The English housecarls and fyrdmen, with persistence and superior numbers, ground down the invaders. By dusk all organised resistance to the English assault had ended and the Norse survivors of the enormously bloody contest were desperately fleeing for their boats at Riccall.

The Norsemen's army had been smashed. Their invasion had been defeated, their chief leaders slain. The dead included not only Harald Hardrada and Tostig, but also Eystein Orre and his brother Nicholas and the Irish king whom Hardrada had enlisted and hundreds of Norwegian thanes and military and political leaders who had joined the adventure. The battle just ended at Stamford Bridge had been an enormous disaster for them and for their country, and an immense victory for King Harold and England and for the thousands of English fighting men who had answered King Harold's call to arms, a horrifyingly large number of whom had given up their lives in their country's defence.

Long before any fleeing survivors could reach Riccall, King Harold's mounted housecarls overtook them and forced their surrender, taking them captive and holding them to await the king's justice. Among them were the Orkney earls, the brothers Paul and Erlend Torfinnson, and Copsig, Tostig's loyal lieutenant. Captured beside the ships at Riccall were Hardrada's young son, Prince Olaf, and Tostig's sons, Skule and Ketel. They would have to face the king their fathers had sought to destroy.

Harold would be solemn as his nephews stood before him in the earl's palace in York. They were solemn, too, having no idea what the king would do with them but undoubtedly fearing the worst.

Harold ended up letting the boys know that he didn't want to punish them for what their father had done. Their father had paid with his life, and that was penalty enough for his crimes. He would tell them that they were free to go back to their mother and their grandfather and that perhaps someday they would return to England.

Young Prince Olaf had no advantage of kinship to King Harold and was likely more fearful than Tostig's sons had been in standing before the king in York. Olaf was a royal prince, a presumptive leader of the nation that had made war against the English king and the English people. Olaf probably felt he would be held responsible, and he likely was very much afraid that he'd never see home again.

Olaf confessed his participation in the wrong done and begged forgiveness and mercy. He offered reparations and tribute.

Harold was persuaded. He granted Olaf mercy and told him that payment of reparations and the giving of hostages would be worked out. Except for those hostages, the young prince was told, he and his men were free to return home.

The Norsemen, led by their suddenly matured prince, returned to their ships at Riccall, carrying their wounded aboard their vessels. They manned their oars and glided soberly down the River Ouse, back toward the sea, headed for home. They had come in 300 ships. They were leaving in twenty-four – an indication of the awful loss they had suffered at Stamford Bridge.

Among those who sailed for home that day were the Orkney earls, Paul and Erlend Torfinnson. Days later, when the flotilla carrying the Norse survivors of Stamford Bridge reached the Orkneys, the Torfinnson brothers learned that on the same day and at about the same hour that her father had died in combat, Princess Maria, Hardrada's beloved eldest and favourite child, had died of an illness, thought to have been pneumonia.

Meanwhile, King Harold and the remainder of his valiant army, those who had escaped death in the great victory at Stamford Bridge, rested and recuperated at York, any thoughts of Duke William and a Norman army too hard to bear for now.

17

THE NORMAN FLEET

SEPTEMBER 1066

Duke William had been ready to sail since the middle of August. He had ships enough to go, but the wind was wrong, and he was left waiting in frustration.

Unbelievably, considering the short time in which he had done it, the duke had assembled a fleet of some 700 vessels, most of them expressly built for the invasion. Most were forty to fifty feet in length, eight to twelve feet in the beam, lapstrake, deckless, propelled by a single sail and designed to carry men, horses, equipment and supplies – as many and as much as possible. Oars and rowers took up too much space, and so the boats had none. The advantages of the invasion ships were that they could be built quickly and could transport maximum loads for their size. Their disadvantages were that, open to weather and the sea, they were vulnerable to stormy conditions at sea and were completely dependent on a favourable wind.

The wind in August was unfavourable. Oddly, for the time of year, it had kept coming from the north-east, into the face of the fleet, massed in the Dives estuary, its crews restlessly waiting for the wind to turn and blow from the south and drive them north across the Channel. Except for horses and men, the ships were loaded, ready to go at the first promising sign of a change in the wind.

When Duchess Matilda came from Rouen to see William at his headquarters at the mouth of the Dives, and to inspect William's flagship, *Mora*, her contribution to the campaign, she found him impatient and eager. There was no question of postponement, however. The duke realised that if he didn't go this year, there would be no next year for his campaign. He knew he would never again be able to put together an army like this one. The mercenaries he had enlisted, he feared, would start deserting if they had to wait much longer. A few had already left. Once they were gone, they were probably gone for good.

There were other considerations. His army was running out of provisions. Idle and bored men, particularly hungry men, were difficult to control, and discipline and morale were becoming hard to maintain. If the invasion were postponed till next year, Harold's position would be stronger. He would be harder to defeat. And perhaps most decisive in his thoughts was the realisation that he would seem a fool for having announced that he was going, then failing to go. He would not stand for seeming a fool. For all those reasons, it was now or never.

He was no doubt glad to see Matilda. For one thing, he had instructions he wanted to give her. He told her that he wanted her to bring their children to him there. He didn't want to go to Rouen to see them because he was afraid the wind would shift while he was gone and he would not be able to take immediate advantage of the change. But he did want to see the children before he left for England.

The children came, and William told them what he wanted them to know. In particular, he told fourteen-year-old Robert, his eldest, that he was counting on him to fill in for him while he was gone. Matilda would actually be in charge, but Robert was the heir apparent, and William wanted him to feel the weight of responsibility, which would quickly increase if William did not return.

On Tuesday 12 September, the wind began blowing from the southwest. The great campaign to conquer England was finally about to get under way.

By mid-afternoon the cavalrymen's horses, some 3,000 of them, had been led across gangplanks and into their transports, the most delicate part of the embarkation, and Duke William's army of Normans and their allies, some 12,000 strong, had boarded their vessels and found cramped spots in which to sit and endure the 110-mile voyage to their landing zone on the English coast. Their ships loaded, the crews – the professional sailors among the duke's invasion force – raised their sails, cast off their mooring lines and, lining up their vessels in long files behind the *Mora*, the largest vessel in the fleet, sailed smartly out of the Dives estuary and into the Bay of the Seine, bound for England, the wind brisk and warm at their backs, the sea choppy and wide before them, the 700 sails and moving ships an awesome sight to the hundreds who stood on the shore and watched.

Three hours later, at dusk, the weather began to change. The winds increased and slowly shifted from south-westerly to westerly, rushing in wildly from the Atlantic, carrying gales and torrential rain, roiling the sea and driving huge billows broadsides into the struggling vessels of the Norman fleet.

Duke William had ordered a lighted lantern hoisted atop the *Mora's* mast, so his crews could identify the fleet's lead ship in the dark, and now that light became a moving beacon in the stormy blackness, going with the wind, shifting the fleet's course from north-east to east. The ship's steering oar became useless. The wind was in control now, and there was no way of knowing where it was taking *Mora* and the rest of the fleet, except that it was somewhere to the east.

The light of Wednesday 13 September found the fleet, battered and decimated, in the refuge of the Bay of the Somme, at St Valery, in Ponthieu. It had been blown past one hundred miles of the Normandy and Ponthieu coastlines before finding safe harbour. And now the wind streamed again from the north.

The duke ordered a quick muster, which revealed alarming news. Ships had been lost to the storm, capsized or swamped in the tempest, and lost also to the desertion of their crews and the frightened and disheartened mercenaries who had been their passengers. The total number of his losses the duke was unwilling to say. To hide the losses from his men and from the Norman people, William ordered reconnaissance patrols to backtrack along the shoreline and recover the bodies of the drowned that had washed up on the beaches and immediately bury them. The surviving deserters he would deal with later.

To conceal the loss of supplies in the storm, William ordered rations increased for his troops. Meanwhile, the wind kept blowing from the north.

The town of St Valery had been named for Walaric (or Valery, as later French-speakers spelled the name), a seventh-century French monk whose horticultural research yielded marvels in insect-resistant produce and gained for him a legendary status. He later became an evangelist, then still later he moved to a place near the mouth of the River Somme and for a while lived as a hermit, until he began attracting disciples who wanted to learn from him, whereupon he founded a monastery to house and nurture them, spiritually and otherwise. While there, he also led a campaign to evangelise the people of the Pas de Calais area and converted a great many pagans to Christianity. The monastery he founded eventually came to be called the St Valery-sur-Somme Abbey, and the nearby little town took the name St Valery-sur-Somme for itself as well.

After his death in AD 620, Valery's body was interred in a shrine in the abbey minster, and the locals, who venerated him, came to it to pray and to seek healing for themselves and their loved ones. Over time, many miracles were attributed to Valery. A sort of cult developed around him, with a large number of followers who believed the invocation of his spirit could produce wondrous occurrences.

After two weeks in the port of St Valery, Duke William, desperate for a change in the direction of the wind and increasingly frustrated by the inefficacy of his own prayers and those of his priests and associates, decided to enlist the help of St Valery himself. He ordered the casket containing Valery's remains to be removed from its shrine and carried down onto the flats beside the mouth of the Somme, below the town of St Valery, and placed there on a carpet that had been laid on the ground for that purpose. Around the casket he assembled his army in unit formations, and a special prayer service began. While the entire invasion army knelt around Valery's casket, Duke William's spokesmen and William himself beseeched, begged, implored and importuned, in the name of St Valery, for God to intervene and cause a favourable wind. Many of the troops brought cash and other offerings forward and left them beside the casket. It was a gigantic spectacle. Then Valery's remains and the offerings were solemnly returned to the shrine in the abbey minster.

On Wednesday 27 September, a few days after the special prayer meeting, while Duke William expectantly watched, the weathervane atop the steeple of the abbey minster swung around to point a new direction for the wind. No longer was it coming from the north. It was blowing directly out of the south, warm and fair.

The ships were immediately reloaded, provisions, equipment and horses placed swiftly aboard. Duke William conducted a hastily called, hurried but thorough operations meeting with his commanders and then, probably with fitz Osbern, Odo and Robert, he boarded the *Mora* and ordered the ship's captain, Stephen, to sail immediately, north by west, to the far shore of La Manche.

It was late in the afternoon by the time the fleet sailed out of the Bay of the Somme, with daylight already merging into autumn twilight. Sunset would be at 5.34 p.m. The fleet had sixty miles of sea to cross, which amounted to twelve to fifteen hours of sailing time, given the fair wind at their backs. Most of the voyage would be made in darkness, a danger that William told his commanders was actually an advantage.

The darkness would in some ways make the crossing more difficult, he granted, particularly in trying to keep the fleet together. But in the dark they would not be noticed by Harold's fleet. They would not have to run the risk of being engaged before they landed. What he wanted, what he was eager for, was a land battle, not a sea battle. Now he and his fleet were setting sail to find it.

18

THE PEVENSEY LANDING
SEPTEMBER 1066

As twilight deepened, Duke William ordered the lighted lantern raised again atop *Mora*'s mast to guide the fleet, and in the darkening night the lantern's light and a crescent moon were the only brightness that the huddled Norman troops could see as they sat in their boats in the damp and darkness, waiting for the long, slow hours of the voyage to pass. When the moon disappeared at 9.15 p.m., the lantern at *Mora*'s masthead became a lone and tiny star in an immense black universe.

The plan was for the fleet to follow the pinpoint of lantern light for about ten hours, which should place the vessels some eight miles or more from the English coast. *Mora* would signal with its light and a trumpet, then all ships of the fleet were to heave to and anchor. Shortly after dawn, with sight of its lead vessel regained, the ships of the fleet would hoist their sails and proceed on to the English coast, following *Mora*. The idea was to avoid making landfall or trying to disembark in the early morning darkness. Duke William had warned his ship captains and his troop commanders that it was absolutely vital that the invasion army go ashore as one massive force, not in small units scattered along the coast, isolated groups that could be overwhelmed by English coast guards and armed civilians. In his operations meetings William had doubtlessly emphasised to his commanders the importance of staying together.

About 2.30 a.m. *Mora*'s captain signalled the halt. As the hours crept by, the ships' crews tried to sleep through their anxiety over where they were and how close they were to the other vessels, while the troops tried to sleep through their seasickness, and the pages, without sleep, fought to control the restive horses, grown dangerously skittish with the hours of pitching and tossing on the open sea.

Dawn broke at 5 a.m. The new day was Thursday 28 September. Perhaps awake while the blackness softened into grey at the sun's first light, Duke William would eagerly peer over *Mora*'s stern and sides, into the space where the other ships should be. He saw nothing but grey mist, however, and heard nothing but the lap of the waves against *Mora*'s hull.

Mora's captain ordered a man aloft to see what he could from the masthead. He saw nothing. Bigger, faster and carrying more sail and less burden, William's flagship had apparently outrun the rest of the fleet and lost contact.

According to one Norman account of events, it was then that the duke ordered breakfast served and leisurely ate it, determinedly showing no sign of anxiety or doubt that his fleet would soon appear through the mists.

When his breakfast was finished, a new report came from the lookout atop *Mora*'s mast. Sails were in sight. Four of them. Minutes later there were too many to count. Duke William told his captain, Stephen, to get under way.

On the captain's orders, the *Mora*'s crew raised the ship's anchor and hoisted its sail, and the entire Norman fleet, its sails clouding the southern horizon, followed its flagship, the wind still fair from the south, the course of all vessels set toward the chalky heights of Beachy Head.

The sun rose at 6.40 a.m., and by the time it burst the morning mist, creeping steadily upward in a clear sky, the men aboard *Mora* had sighted the Sussex shore. The high, white cliffs of Beachy Head, a landmark familiar to all sailors of the English Channel, lay ahead and to the fleet's left, though still far in the distance. The goal was in sight.

In 1066 the town of Pevensey sat on the point of a three-mile-long peninsula that jutted eastward, with the Channel to its south and east, and the odd-shaped tidal lagoon that formed Pevensey harbour to its north and west. The ruins of Anderida, the fortress that the Romans had built to protect the harbour, but which had been overcome and destroyed by Saxon hordes in the sixth century, still stood, its surviving walls twenty-five feet high in places. Beside the ruined Roman fortress the Saxons had founded the town of Pevensey, a seaport and small commercial centre. From Pevensey a road built by the Romans led westward to Lewes and northward via Lewes to London.

Beachy Head, the mariners' towering natural landmark, lay about seven miles down the Channel coast, south-west of Pevensey. Eastward from Pevensey, across its expansive harbour and up the Channel coast, stood the town of Bexhill. On the other side of Bexhill, farther up the Channel coast, lay the inlet that was Bulverhythe harbour, and just beyond it was the seaport of Hastings, with its own small bay that provided a harbour.

Hastings was a place that Duke William knew something about, one of the few such places in all of England. Hastings had been included in the grant that the late King Edward had made to endow the abbey in the Norman city of Fécamp, the controversial gift that continued to irritate Englishmen, particularly King Harold. Some of the monks from the Fécamp abbey on more than one occasion had toured its English estate, which extended from a point west of Hastings eastward to Winchelsea and north to the River Brede. Those monks had come to know the area well and they had no doubt briefed Duke William about it in meetings with the abbey's abbot.

Hastings met William's criteria for a landing site, some more so than others. It was reasonably close to Normandy, less than 120 miles from the original embarkation site at the mouth of the River Dives and about sixty miles from St Valery. The surrounding flat terrain and nearby shingle beaches and its sheltered harbours, its own and the nearby estuary of the River Bulverhythe as well, were suitable for the disembarkation. It was away from known fortifications, such as those presented by the guarded ports of Romney, Dover and Sandwich farther east, all of which had permanent defence forces.

Situated between the harbour of the Bulverhythe, which extended some three miles inland, and the River Brede's estuary, which extended some eight miles inland, to the east and the north, the area around Hastings was suitably defensible from a land attack. And sitting at the lower edge of a wide, fifty-square-mile peninsula that was well farmed, it was also forageable, though not adequate to feed a large army for long.

The Hastings area was the landing zone William had chosen, but Hastings was without a landmark to distinguish it, making the task of sailing directly to it an extremely difficult assignment, even for Stephen, the *Mora*'s captain, who had a reputation as one of the best navigators available and had got the job because of that reputation. The high, white cliffs of Beachy Head were what Stephen and the rest of William's captains had been aiming for. They had been headed on a course of deliberate error, to be corrected when the landmark cliffs were sighted.

Pevensey, however, would now have to be the landing site, since the wind, straight out of the south, would not allow the captains to turn north-eastward to correct their course and sail on to Hastings. As the fleet followed in its wake, *Mora*, with Duke William and perhaps his chief lieutenants aboard, was going to land some ten miles west of the intended landing zone.

At 9 a.m., on a rising tide, *Mora* and the vessels immediately aft of her sailed into the lagoon, with the stony Pevensey shore to port and, across the miles-wide mouth of the lagoon, marshy lowlands to starboard. Within minutes the troop-laden ships ran up on the Pevensey beaches, side by side, one after another, crowding the water's edge with a long, tight line of invasion craft, from which armed troops instantly began spilling feet first into the chill water.

First out of the ships were Duke William's archers, their bows strung tight, quivers full, alert, moving quickly into skirmish formation, ready to release a storm of arrows upon anyone they found to oppose them. They set off in two directions, up and down the beach, searching for an opposing force. They found none.

Then came the chevaliers, assisted by their pages, coaxing and prodding their huge war horses up the ships' gangways, then down into the shallow surf, then leading them up onto the beaches, the horses stepping gingerly over the rocks. In full battledress, wearing their hauberks and helmets, shields slung from their necks, swords at their waists, lances in their hands, the chevaliers mounted their horses and assembled into a massive cavalry formation on the beach. On a series of commands, shouted up and down the beach, the mounted chevaliers advanced in wide ranks across the beach and into the town, from which most of the inhabitants, upon seeing the huge fleet approach, had swiftly fled and which now lay virtually empty of life.

While the chevaliers then organised into reconnaissance patrols to fan out into the surrounding countryside, the bulk of Duke William's army, the infantrymen, poured from their ships and quickly occupied the town and established a perimeter defence.

Once the beach and the town of Pevensey were secure, William's engineers unloaded one of three prefabricated wooden forts they had brought with them and began assembling it within the broken walls of the Romans' old Anderida.

William himself, among the first Normans to hit the beach, had suffered an embarrassing misstep as he trudged through the surf. He had broken his fall with his hands, then straightened again, his arms soaked and his wet hands clenched into fists.

The duke raised his hands and displayed the wet sand he was holding in them. 'God be praised!' he shouted. 'Today I have seized the soil of England!'

The next day, Friday 29 September, William put one of his barons, Humphrey of Tilleul, in command of a unit to guard the fort that was still under construction, while William and his cavalry struck out overland for Hastings. They would follow the lagoon's shoreline as it bent north-westward, then northward, and then the column would proceed eastward for about six miles, then south to Hastings, a march totalling some thirty miles. The foot soldiers would take a more direct, shorter route. They were ferried across the mouth of the lagoon to land on the marshy western edge of the Hastings peninsula and from there they would march to Hastings, about ten miles to the east. The ships laden with supplies and equipment were to sail out of Pevensey Harbour on an ebbing tide and with a favourable wind sail to Hastings.

To feed themselves, the army would forage and pillage, seizing the cattle and stores of English farmers, merchants and villagers as they pressed on to Hastings. William ordered his commanders to have the men fend for themselves and take from the Saxons whatever they needed. If the Saxons resisted, they would deserve whatever the Normans did to them. Anyone, any group, any town that resisted, the duke declared, was to receive no mercy. If the inhabitants co-operated and submitted, the commanders were permitted to grant quarter, using their own judgement.

As the two columns pressed toward Hastings, the Norman cavalrymen nearly wiped out the towns of Hailsham, Herstmonceux and

Hooe and ravaged the countryside between, burning houses and barns, murdering farmers and villagers while women and children looked on helplessly or fled in horror to seek refuge in cemeteries, in vain in many cases. The town of Ashburnham was obliterated, burned to the ground, its citizens slaughtered. Beyond it to the east, Ninfield and Catsfield, north-west of Hastings, were severely damaged and many of its people slaughtered.

The Norman infantrymen stormed ashore just west of Bexhill and engulfed the town, completely destroying it and routing or slaughtering its citizens. The column, following the shoreline of the Bulverhythe harbour, then marched on Crowhurst, Wilting and Filsham, laying them all waste, burning, looting and murdering, cutting a wide path of devastation and terror as they marched irresistibly on toward Hastings, where they would rejoin Duke William's force of mounted chevaliers.

The city of Hastings, in the face of such an awesome armed force, submitted without a blow being struck. William received the surrender from the city's burgesses, and his troops quickly set about occupying the city while his transports, carrying supplies and equipment, now safely entered the harbours and were unloaded.

Using workers conscripted from among Hastings' citizens, William's engineers erected the second of their prefabricated forts and surrounded it with a trench and a palisade. William established a headquarters inside the fort, which was situated on a hilltop overlooking two valleys that led northward – in the direction that King Harold's English army must come.

That done, William ordered his army to stand for inspection and when it had assembled in a massive formation, he reviewed his troops from horseback. Satisfied they were ready to do battle, he sent an envoy to London with a message for King Harold, then began his wait to see what Harold would do.

19
THE OMEN
OCTOBER 1066

Leaving the worst of the wounded behind in York, Harold and his diminished army set out for London within days after their victory at Stamford Bridge, moving briskly in a long column, banners flying, spirits high following the triumph over the Norsemen.

The victory had been costly, however, and not just in fyrdmen. The housecarls particularly had suffered severe losses. Many of Harold's very best professional soldiers had given their lives, and the army that he was now leading southward was not the same as had faced Harald Hardrada and Tostig the previous Monday. Tostig hadn't succeeded in removing Harold from the throne, but he had made him pay dearly for keeping it. And he had left in Harold's mind another haunting memory. Tostig had been cut down within Harold's sight.

On Sunday 1 October, while *en route* to London and riding with the lead elements of his army, Harold was approached by a small group of horsemen riding hard toward him, coming from the south.

The riders drew up their mounts within hailing distance of the first ranks of the army's column and delivered their dreaded message. The Normans had landed at Pevensey, on Thursday last.

Harold quickly decided to take his bodyguard and ride swiftly for London. He wouldn't wait for the rest of the troops. They would catch up with him in London and, as they moved toward London, their commanders would seek to enlist every able-bodied man they could find.

When Harold reached London on Thursday 5 October, more bad news was awaiting him. Reports had come to London that Duke William's troops had swept eastward from Pevensey to Hastings, occupying and fortifying Hastings, looting the countryside and leaving it in flames, murdering the inhabitants in a pitiless assault.

He decided to march to Hastings as soon as the column reached London and he began recalling the fyrd from Kent and from Sussex and from anywhere else they could be found to marshal within the next few days.

There was one piece of good news. Two of William's ships had strayed from the rest of the fleet in the channel and landed at Romney. The coast defence force at Romney had wiped them out, to a man.

The next day Harold received more news. William had sent an envoy with a message for him. He was a monk who spoke English, Hugh Margot of the Fécamp abbey. When Harold received him, he asked if Harold had forgotten the oath he had sworn to the duke, a solemn promise to be his liegeman and to serve him in England. Harold probably told the monk that since then he had sworn a new oath, and it was to drive the Bastard and his army back to the foreign shores from which they came – or else to bury them beneath English soil.

Margot told him he still had time to save himself, to rectify his wrongs, if he would repent and keep the oath sworn to Duke William and to God. It was not merely his life that was in peril, the monk told him. His immortal soul was in jeopardy. His holiness the Pope, the monk told Harold, was excommunicating him. A hearing had already been held in Rome, Harold was told, and he been adjudicated as guilty.

His holiness, Margot said, had pronounced his blessing upon Duke William's campaign and declared it a holy cause. That being the case, Harold would not be merely fighting a man, Margot told him. He would be fighting the Church. He would be fighting God. If Harold doubted the monk, he would have proof enough when Harold would see Duke William coming to him in battle beneath the Pope's banner, with holy relics about his neck and the Pope's ring containing the sacred relic of St Peter on his hand. Duke William's cause was a holy cause, Harold was told, and he was damning himself by contending it. What was more, he was damning all who followed him into battle against William's holy cause.

Margot urged Harold to repent before it was too late. He said the duke, a godly and merciful man, was ready to grant mercy if Harold would give back what he had usurped. If not, the duke would be merciless.

Harold refused. He knew about the Bastard's mercy. It had been displayed in Norman savagery from Pevensey to Hastings and it was no better than the duke's wrath. Harold is likely to have told the monk to tell his master the duke that he, Harold, stood ready to answer to God, not William, and that God alone would decide who was in the right and who was not.

Harold's brother Earl Gyrth believed he had the answer to the threat of excommunication. The Pope was excommunicating Harold and all who would follow him into battle. The proposed solution was to not have anyone follow Harold into battle. Have them follow Gyrth. Gyrth hadn't been excommunicated. No one would be damned for following him. If Harold's great sin was that he had sworn on holy relics to support the Bastard, Gyrth would avoid the penalty for Harold. Gyrth hadn't sworn or promised anything. No sacred vow would be broken if he took the army against William.

Harold, however, was not persuaded. It was his fight, he insisted, and the Bastard was *his* enemy. He would evade neither one.

Gyrth had another argument to offer. There was more than one reason for Harold's turning over leadership of the army now. If Harold were to be killed in combat, Gyrth argued, England would have lost its king. On the other hand, if Gyrth were to lead the army and be killed, England would have lost only a general. Gyrth was expendable. Harold was not. Battles could be lost. Men could be lost. The king must *not* be lost.

Harold still refused.

By now Gyrth may have decided that it was a trial by ordeal that Harold sought. Harold versus William – and may God decide the victor. To a reasonable man it must have seemed outrageously, foolishly reckless. It seemed as if Harold were testing not himself but God, as if he were forcing the Almighty to choose between him and William.

Harold rejected all of Gyrth's protestations. He had decided. He was determined to fight the Bastard. He let Gyrth and Leofwine know that that was the way it was going to be.

Harold continued with his plan to move out of London the following week, as soon as the remainder of his troops arrived from York and his army was reassembled in London. Gyrth advised that it would be wiser to wait till the entire fyrd could be mustered, from all the shires. With those men, Harold would have three times the number that he would have with only the men returning from York.

But Harold evidently didn't want to wait any longer than absolutely necessary. He wanted to contain William and keep him from ravaging any more of the country, or occupying some sizable piece of England and holding it hostage. He didn't want to have to negotiate with the Bastard. Within a week, Harold judged, he would have enough of an army to accomplish what he wanted. He decided he would wait no longer than that.

A dozen miles north of London, beside the grassy banks of the River Lea at Waltham, stood the church that had been erected by one of King Canute's devout lieutenants, Tofig the Proud, to house and memorialise the stone crucifix, or rood, that, according to legend, he had found buried some sixty feet deep after its location had been revealed to him in a dream. The church and its rood had become a shrine over the years, attracting a great many who sought healing or other help.

When Tofig died, King Edward expropriated the town of Waltham and the area around it, which Tofig had owned and which included the church that Tofig had built. At first, Edward made Waltham a property of the Crown, but he later awarded it to Harold, when Harold was earl of East Anglia.

The church and the land around it became one of Harold's favourite places, and he hired builders to expand and beautify the structure. He decided to establish a seminary alongside it, to train young men for the priesthood. He dedicated some of his lands to endow the seminary and he hired a faculty and staff of canons to run it. To be its chancellor Harold appointed a scholar from the Continent, a man named Adelhard, who was also a physician and who had once treated Harold for a paralysis of his leg. When Adelhard's treatments had failed to cure Harold, Adelhard had urged him to seek help at Waltham's shrine of the rood, whose curative power, he said, had worked for many others.

Eager for relief, Harold had tried it, visiting the shrine and praying earnestly before the crucifix, its stone Christ figure overlaid with silver. Remarkably, Harold's condition began to improve and the ailment eventually disappeared. That experience inspired in Harold an even deeper devotion to the Waltham abbey and its rood, so much so that he often would have his men shout, 'Holy cross!' as they plunged into battle, hoping to invoke the power that had cured him and helped so many others.

Now, while he awaited the remarshalling of his army and prepared for the confrontation with William and his invasion force, Harold slipped out of Westminster with his bodyguard and rode to the Waltham abbey and the shrine of the holy rood. On his arrival in Waltham, the abbey's canons escorted him to the church and ushered him inside the ornate sanctuary, the October sun brightening the colourful wall tapestries and filling the high-ceilinged chamber with warmth. He stopped before the main altar and looked up at the silvery figure of Christ upon the cross.

King Harold dropped to his knees and as he clasped his hands in front of him he looked into the face of the Christ figure and began to pray. Moments passed into long minutes as he remained on his knees with his eyes closed and his head bowed. After a long while, he crossed himself, then rose to his feet. He walked forward to the cross and held his hand to it briefly, then prostrated himself and began praying again.

Standing at the rear of the sanctuary were the church's sacristan and the canons who had escorted the king into the church. They were watching him as he prayed before the rood. While he remained prostrate, his head and eyes to the floor, the sacristan and the other canons watching, suddenly, according to their later testimony, they noticed the Christ figure's head move. They watched awestruck as the head slowly slumped forward, as if bowing in reverence or in sorrow. Minutes passed, and the Christ figure's head remained bowed. Finally Harold lifted himself and stood, crossed himself once more, turned around and strode up the centre aisle toward the doors, the canons silently falling in behind him and filing out of the sanctuary, leaving behind the bowed head that would never raise again.

Outside, Harold and his bodyguard heaved themselves onto their mounts, bade the canons goodbye and rode quickly back to Westminster, unaware of the queer occurrence and what, if anything, it might mean to them.

20

THE OPPOSING HILLS
12 OCTOBER–14 OCTOBER 1066

Shortly after dawn on Thursday 12 October, King Harold's army began forming outside the walls of London. Mounted house-carls, survivors of the battle at Stamford Bridge, moved into the first ranks of the coalescing column. They were the men of the standing armies of Earls Gyrth, Leofwine and Waltheof and of Harold's Wessex earldom as well as Harold's royal housecarls, altogether some 2,000 troops.

Forming up behind the housecarls were thanes and fyrdmen, many of them also on horseback, men who had fought at Stamford Bridge and then had hurried south in the rear of King Harold's train as he raced from Northumbria. Other fyrdmen who had fought at Stamford Bridge were still arriving from York, nearly hourly, most of them on foot, some of them walking wounded. Among those fyrdmen were some members of Harold's meagre force of archers. Still other members of the fyrd falling into the formation were men who had joined the column of marchers as it moved southward from York, and there were also those fyrdmen who had been called up within the past few days, coming from the shires within quick marching distance of London.

Many of the fyrdmen, still arriving on foot and on horseback, came wearing their byrnies, waist-length or knee-length, carrying round, wood-frame shields and armed with axes, spears and swords. Others came armoured with nothing more than leather coats and caps, and armed only with scythes, hammers, hatchets, clubs and slings. A few of them came with bows and arrows. All counted, the men of the fyrd numbered some 6,000 fighters.

Among Harold's commanders, besides his brothers and Waltheof, were Ansgar, who was the grandson of Tofig the Proud and was sheriff of Middlesex; Godric, the sheriff of Berkshire; and Thurkill, a leading landowner of Berkshire. Harold's ageing uncle, Aelfwig, brother of Earl Godwin and abbot of the minster at Winchester, had also reported for duty, bringing twelve men of his order to join Harold's army. Harold still had not heard from the Earls Morkere and Edwin since the debacle at Gate Fulford.

By mid-morning the leading elements of the column had moved out, heading south-east toward Crayford, roughly paralleling the course of the Thames, following the old Roman road. The route from London to Hastings, covering more than sixty miles, passed through Crayford, then led to Rochester, where the column would turn south-ward and cross the River Medway, then on to Maidstone. Hastings lay almost due south of Maidstone, about thirty miles distant, beyond the thick oak forest of the Andreadsweald. Harold sped ahead with his mounted housecarls, the sooner to get the lay of the land and choose the battle site, and the rest of the army would follow. Fresh fyrd units would join Harold's force outside Hastings, arriving from places east and west of the army's line of march. The assembly point, where all ele-ments of Harold's army were to meet, was Caldbec Hill, distinguished by a huge and ancient apple tree that grew near the top of it, known as the hoar apple tree, a landmark familiar to many in Harold's army.

At Sedlescombe, about six miles north of Hastings, the old Roman road from Rochester to Hastings crossed the River Brede, named for its breadth, which was about 200 yards at Sedlescombe. Travellers at that point had to take a ferry to reach the other side. Harold had decided a ferry crossing was impractical for his army and when he neared Sedlescombe on Friday 13 October, the second day of his march, having encamped the first night outside Maidstone, he wheeled his column toward the south-west along a narrow trackway that dated from Celtic times and ran along a wooded ridge to points where the Brede was shallow enough to ford. The trackway forked at Caldbec

Hill, its west branch leading to the old Lewes-London road and its east branch leading back to the Hastings-Rochester road, rejoining it at a point south of the Brede. For William to move his army from Hastings toward the English interior, Harold knew, it would be necessary for him to come past Caldbec Hill.

Early on Friday evening Harold and the housecarls, near exhaustion after their hurried ride of two long days, drew up to the rendezvous point on the slopes of Caldbec Hill. Within sight of the hoar apple tree, the housecarls dismounted to rest and to await the arrival of the fyrd-men, some already beginning to straggle in. While his troops rested, Harold and his brothers, in the fading light, reconnoitred the nearby surrounding country.

For nearly two weeks Duke William had been holed up in his rustic, prefabricated fort on the outskirts of Hastings. Some of his chief lieutenants were growing impatient. Like William's mercenaries and fortune-seekers, restlessly idling like garrison soldiers in and around Hastings, but held in check by the duke's stern discipline, they were eager for more action than foraging, patrolling and drilling provided.

If anyone among his closest lieutenants was bold enough to question the duke about the delay, he probably would have given his reason for not pushing farther inland. They were still there in Hastings, he likely explained, because they were waiting for Harold to come to them. Since he hadn't yet come, they continued to wait. If asked how he could be sure that Harold would come, William probably replied that he knew he would come because it was Harold's nature to respond directly, that Harold was a man of immediate action, of impulse even. William felt he knew Harold. He had seen him act. Harold was not subtle; he was not devious; and he was not afraid. He would come.

By now William probably would have learned of Harold's battle at Stamford Bridge. He would have known that Harold's army had suffered significant losses in that battle.

On Friday evening all doubt of Harold's intentions was erased. A Norman mounted patrol brought the news to the duke that the Saxon army had arrived. It was at the prominence of Caldbec Hill.

The wait was over.

William ordered a special Mass to be held that evening and he commanded his entire army, except for sentries and patrols, to assemble for the service.

King Harold's reconnaissance had discovered that from Caldbec Hill, which rose to a height of some 350 feet, the ground quickly sloped down more than a hundred feet on the south side and then rose again to form a ridge that ran roughly east and west, then dipped again and formed a saddle between the ridge on the north and Telham Hill on the south, the two elevations about 500 yards apart. Beyond Telham Hill to the south lay Hastings, about five miles distant. East and west of the saddle, streams flowed away from it, in opposite directions, and the ground around the streams was marshy, particularly on the west side. Through the saddle, crossing it from south-east to north-west on high ground that lay between the marshy areas, ran the track that led to and from Hastings, the route that William would have to take.

On the slopes of Caldbec Hill the weary troops of Harold's army, exhausted after their long and hurried march, had wrapped their cloaks and blankets around themselves and, with their armour and weapons beside them, had stretched out on the ground to sleep even while twilight still dimly lit the sky. Other fighters, fyrdmen newly called from their farms and villages and fyrdmen who had travelled from London on foot, continued to arrive in small groups until total darkness enveloped the countryside.

While his troops rested, Harold would meet with his commanders by firelight at his command post at the foot of Caldbec Hill, to eat and to go over the king's plan. He would explain that they now sat within hours of the Bastard's army and that they would take the fight to the Normans when Harold and his army were ready. The English fleet, he would explain, would be lying off the coast of Hastings by now, and there would be no retreat for the Bastard and his alien horde. Harold planned to advance on him and do the same as he had done to Hardrada. If William tried to break out, the English forces would block his movement with a position athwart his northward route. 'God is with us!' he would declare reassuringly as he dismissed the commanders.

The commanders would rise to their feet and shout their response in unison, 'God is with us!'

The first grey light of dawn on Saturday 14 October began seeping into the early morning darkness around half past five while a waning but brilliant two-thirds moon still hung high in the nearly cloudless sky. The air was damp and cool, but the morning was without a sign of rain. Duke William had already decided and told his commanders that if the morning brought rain, he would try to delay the battle for a day, since a ground-soaking rain would render his cavalry ineffectual on the soggy turf and take away the advantage he believed his cavalry gave him.

When he awoke and saw no rain in the brightening sky, he doubtless made a mental note that this was a good sign.

Even before first light, the duke's troops had risen and were preparing to begin their march. About 6 a.m., with sunrise still twenty minutes away, the lead elements of the column, the chevaliers and archers, formed up and started moving out. The chevaliers led their horses, their heavy hauberks thrown across their mounts' saddles. Many of the foot soldiers had placed their armour in carts, farther back in the column. When the battle became imminent, chevaliers and infantrymen would halt and put on their armour.

The column stretched out to a length of some three miles and moved steadily northward from Hastings along a ridge from which wooded slopes fell away on either side, giving protection to the column's flanks.

At the head of the column Duke William rode on the black charger given to him by King Alfonso of Aragon. Behind William, toward the rear of the column, three more of the duke's horses, each accoutred for battle, were being led, the duke making certain he would stay mounted no matter how many horses were killed or disabled beneath him. William rode with his sword at his waist and carrying a mace in his right hand. Around his neck, like a necklace of bones, he wore the holy relics, the remains of Saints Rasyphus and Ravennus, over which Harold had sworn to be William's liegeman. On his finger he wore the ring given to him and blessed by Pope Alexander II, the ring with the tiny compartment containing the hair believed to have come from the head of St Peter.

After more than an hour of marching, Duke William halted the column for a break. As his chevaliers steadied their horses, the duke, having dismounted, strode back toward the gathering of men and mounts. He stopped and took a position upslope of the troops, facing them. He decided he would give them one more pep talk before ordering them to hurl themselves against the defences of the English army.

When he finished, he gave the order for his troops to put on their armour. The order was passed along the length of the column. While his troops put on their hauberks, pulling them on over their heads like stiff nightshirts, one of the duke's squires trotted up to him with the duke's hauberk and held it up to help ease the duke into it. William ducked his head and lifted the skirt of the hauberk and inserted his head and shoulders into it, then let it fall over his back and belly.

At that point, he realised he had it on backwards. With the help of his squire, he quickly pulled it off over his head, turned it around and tugged it back on again over his thick shoulders and big belly. For the superstitious among his troops who had seen him make the mistake and might take it as a portent, he quickly said in a loud voice, 'Let this be a sign for all of you. Today is a day of turnabout. Whereas I have been till this day a duke, after today I shall be king.' The troops cheered.

At the foot of Caldbec Hill the men of King Harold's English army, having breakfasted on their rations and re-armed themselves, were falling into their unit formations as the sun steadily rose above the treetops of Petley Wood, to the left of their position. Additional fyrd-men, who had set out for the hoar apple tree at the day's first light, were arriving to bolster Harold's numbers. Now, before the troops were to move out, a fast-riding detail of housecarls rode up to Harold's command post from the south and quickly dismounted and gave the king an urgent report.

The Bastard's army was on the march. It was about three miles to the south-east, moving toward them.

Harold turned to his brothers and told them to establish a defensive line on the ridge slightly to his right, the ridge that faced toward Telham Hill. His plan was to take the high ground. The Bastard would have to come uphill to meet them, across the open field that lay between the ridge and Telham Hill. From that position the English would command both the north-south and east-west roads. And from atop the south slope of the ridge Harold and his commanders would be able to observe everything William did.

Perhaps at that point, when Harold halted, as if finished with his orders, Gyrth nodded and put his hand on Harold's shoulder and urged him aside. He would tell him that he didn't mean to seem disagreeable, but that he wanted to be sure that Harold had considered everything. He warned Harold that he was about to wager everything on this one battle. He reminded him that they didn't yet have their whole army there, that fyrdmen were still arriving and would be for the next several days. He likely then repeated his chief concern. Harold himself, the king, the country's leader, authority and chief general, was about to expose himself to the fight. Gyrth could not help telling Harold his worst fear – that something might happen to Harold during the battle. And if he were killed, what then?

Harold, still heedless, evidently shrugged off the caution, perhaps telling Gyrth that they had been through that argument before.

Gyrth again urged Harold to let him take command, earnestly imploring Harold to remove himself from the impending battle. Harold again steadfastly and stubbornly refused. He refused to yield command, refused to retreat, refused to delay. He was determined to stop the Bastard then and there – and, perhaps in his mind, submit himself to God's ordeal.

Gyrth, with far greater foresight than his brother the king, had lost all his arguments.

Harold and his brothers then left the royal pavilion and with the other commanders began ordering the English fighters into formation. The commanders marched their troops some 600 yards to the south, across the ridge and onto its southern slope, facing Telham Hill.

Near the spot where the south-east to north-west trackway crossed it, the ridge gradually rose twenty-five feet or so, then dipped sharply on the east side, forming a hump on the spine of the ridge some 400 yards wide. That peak on the ridge was where Harold would establish his command post, at the centre of the English line and about fifty yards to its rear. It was also where the two trackways intersected. From his command post he would look over the heads of his men and down onto the meadow that extended southward a mile or more, around and past Telham Hill, to the place where the woods north of Hastings began. That area between the edge of the woods on the south and the ridge on the north was part of a Sussex estate known as Santlache, the name's origin lost in the oblivion of prehistory but believed to mean 'sandy stream'. The rise on the ridge, where King Harold would centre his line, was Santlache Hill, later to be corrupted to Senlac Hill.

Harold ordered his commanders to form a line that would extend about 700 yards, from the sharply sloped eastern side of Senlac Hill at its left flank to the lower part of the ridge at the right flank. In front of both flanks were the marshy areas of the streams that flowed to the west and east. The English line presented a front rank of 1,000 men in the close-order formation of the famous, fearsome Saxon shield wall. Behind the front rank stood seven more ranks of 1,000 men each, ready to step up and close any gaps that occurred in the front ranks during battle.

Harold's commanders interspersed groups of housecarls among the fyrdmen in the line, to stiffen it and hold the thanes and fyrdmen steady during the expected onslaught. When the enemy was about to be engaged, the housecarls and the best armed and armoured thanes and fyrdmen would be only inches apart from one another in the front ranks, standing sideways to the assault, shields on one arm to deflect arrows but slung on their backs or stabbed into the ground when both hands gripped their murderous, two-handed battleaxes. By 8 a.m. all were in position.

Near the crest of the hump of the ridge, where he had established his command post and had erected his pavilion, Harold ordered his standard bearers to plant both the dragon of Wessex flag and the Fighting Man, his own personal battle emblem, its primitive, stylised man figure superimposed on a white background. Around Harold a contingent of bodyguards stood to protect the king.

With his troops in position, Harold would now rally them to the cause, telling them they would be fighting not for themselves alone but for their families, their homes, their nation, their independence. 'God is with us!' he would shout up and down the lines of fighters. 'Holy cross!'

The Englishmen in response would raise their shields and weapons above their heads and shout back to their king in a thunderous chorus, 'God is with us! Holy cross!'

As the head of the invaders' column neared the southern slope of Telham Hill, beyond whose crest lay the imposing English line, a mounted scout would ride up to Duke William and give him the latest report. The Saxons were arrayed across the field that lay on the other side of the hill. And Harold himself had come to command. His emblems had been noticed on the top of the far ridge, about fifty yards behind the Saxon lines.

William suddenly dismounted and knelt on the ground in an attitude of prayer. He audibly beseeched God to give him a great victory, and he promised that, when the grant of victory had been received, he would in gratitude turn the site of the battle into holy ground. He swore that he would build a memorial there so that all men would know that God was with him at his hour of triumph.

From the cluster of men standing around the duke, a monk from the Abbey of Marmoutier, William Faber, stepped to the duke's side. He had heard the duke's prayer and he asked the duke if, when the victory was won and William erected a memorial, he would build an abbey on the spot dedicated to the monk's abbey's patron, St Martin of Tours, a man beloved by all in Normandy.

William considered the request, then gave his answer. He would do as the monk asked.

At about nine o'clock that morning, the first Norman troops, mounted chevaliers, topped Telham Hill and came spilling over it, down onto its northern slope. Duke William, astride his black charger, rode with them and, facing the English line some 400 yards in front of him, began directing the deployment of his column into battle formation.

On his left flank the duke placed the division made up mostly of Bretons and commanded by Count Alan of Brittany. On his right flank he placed the division made up of Flemish and French troops, under the command of Count Eustace of Boulogne, assisted by William fitz Osbern. In the centre of the huge formation he placed his own Norman troops, the great bulk of his force. The right half of the Norman division he put under the command of his brother Odo, its left half under the command of his brother Robert.

Each of the three divisions was composed of three separate fighting arms – archers, infantry and cavalry. Across a front as broad as the Saxon shield wall – some 700 yards – William positioned his archery units in the front ranks of the formation, and behind them he placed his infantry units. Behind the infantry he positioned his cavalry.

At about ten o'clock, with all units in position, the duke, on his horse, riding back and forth along the breadth of his ranks, ordered his army to advance, marching *en masse*, keeping the formation intact, moving like a human avalanche down the northern slope of Telham Hill and onto the meadow that spread across the saddle of land between Telham Hill and Senlac Hill. When the front ranks, the archers, were within 150 yards of the English line, and about fifty feet below it, still out of range of King Harold's bowmen, William halted the entire army.

The duke called for his standards, the Leopards of Normandy flag and the traditional Norse raven emblem, as well as the distinctive papal banner emblazoned with a red cross on a white background and with three triangular and knotted tails streaming from one side. To Turstin Rolloson, one of his most trusted knights, the duke handed the Leopards of Normandy flag to bear into the battle. To another trusted knight, Tosteny, the duke gave the papal banner to carry. He instructed them to do the emblems honour and cautioned the two men not to let them fall or be taken.

At about half past ten then, with all in readiness, into the damp but warming autumn air Duke William shouted to his commanders the order to commence the assault.

21

THE BATTLE
14 OCTOBER 1066

The men in the front ranks of King Harold's shield wall grimly watched as the rows of the invaders' archers, most without armour, wearing only leather tunics, stepped out from the mass of foot soldiers and horses and riders, and marched briskly toward the English line, bows gripped in their hands, leather quivers slung from their waists and packed with long, slim, feathered arrows. At a distance of about a hundred yards from the English line, at the maximum effective range of their weapons, the archers halted and fitted arrows onto their bows. They then raised their bows slightly and on a shouted command let loose their tautened bowstrings, launching a deadly flight of steel-pointed arrows straight at the English ranks.

Immediately the wall of English shields rose. Deflected arrows clattered off the tough leather shields; many others struck the English shields head-on, stabbing into them with resounding thuds and sticking to them like long, wooden bristles. The archers quickly and repeatedly reloaded and sent new volleys into the shield wall. Again most of the arrows were deflected or absorbed by the English shields, but with so many hundreds of them shooting into the line, some slipped between shields to find a human mark, and then a deathly moan would rise from a fyrdman with the shaft of an arrow protruding from his throat, or a cry of pain from a man who had taken an arrow in the shoulder. Above the noise, King Harold's commanders shouted encouragement to their troops.

After about fifteen minutes the archery attack ended, the archers' quivers emptied. With so few English bowmen to shoot back and replenish the invaders' arrow supply, Duke William's archers had to fall back to the Norman lines to be resupplied from the wagons on the other side of Telham Hill. Men in the front ranks of the English line, and King Harold from his command post well behind the shield wall, watched as the enemy archers turned and double-timed back to their lines.

Now with the archers having withdrawn to the rear of the invaders' formation, trumpets sounded in the distance, and the mass of enemy foot soldiers moved forward and spread out to form a giant, shallow crescent that, on the shouted commands that carried clearly to the English line, began advancing on the English position, walking at first, then jogging, then as the massive force, four ranks deep, neared the shield wall, breaking into a run, shouting taunts and curses, imprecations and invocations of God's aid, swiftly closing the distance between themselves and the broad, thick wall of English fighting men.

Waiting with chests heaving and heavy breathing, the axemen along the line impaled their shields in the soft turf and grasped their spears to fling into the charging enemy before taking up their broad-bladed, two-handed axes. Swordsmen as well gripped lances and spears, ready to launch them into the attacking mass. The few English bowmen, in position at the rear of the shield wall, were already firing over the heads of their comrades and into the oncoming enemy formation.

Suddenly the leading rank of invaders was but a few yards away, and the English attacked with their lances and spears and stones flung from slings. Here and there the arrows and lances and other projectiles struck home and felled the occasional onrushing soldier, but most were warded off by Norman shields. Within moments the brunt of the invaders' infantry struck the English line, crashing like a human wave against the men of the shield wall, armoured soldiers, their grotesquely helmeted heads and faces up close now, slashing and thrusting at the defenders with swords and spears.

Against the Englishmen's battleaxes neither shield nor armour provided effective defence, and Norman swords were unable to parry the heavy steel axeheads, which cut brutally through metal, leather and wood and chopped into flesh and bone, gashing, smashing and dismembering. The housecarls and thanes in the English front rank efficiently hewed the assaulting infantrymen, severing heads, arms, legs, and inflicting great gaping, bloody wounds, dropping the attackers at the feet of axemen who, when they themselves went down at the edge of a Norman sword, were instantly replaced by the men at their backs.

The English line held and did so with an enormous cost exacted from the invaders' foot soldiers, who scarcely made a dent in the shield wall, much less penetrated it, anywhere along its breadth. On the English right, where Bretons and volunteers from Maine and Anjou had slogged through the edge of the bog and run screaming up the gentle western slope of the ridge, the invaders' losses were particularly heavy. The two front ranks of the shield wall slaughtered the assailants, felling them like saplings, fyrdmen as effective as housecarls in repelling the assault and driving the enemy backward.

All at once then the entire surviving Breton division, the whole of Duke William's left flank, turned around in panic and started running desperately back across the meadow, toward the slope of Telham Hill. From the right side of the English line a deafening chorus of cheers went up when the Englishmen saw the enemy turn tail, and a large unit of fyrdmen, men from the same district, impulsively burst from their positions in the shield wall and, brandishing their weapons and yelling as they ran, pursued the fleeing Bretons down the easy slope of the ridge and past the edge of the boggy area, the swiftest of them overtaking the slowest Bretons and hacking them down.

Hundreds of other fighters on the right side of the shield wall, seeing the chaos and sensing quick victory, then broke from their positions and joined the pursuit, screaming and sprinting toward the fleeing Bretons, the immense noise of their yells drowning out the shouts of their commanders at the rear of the English line, telling them not to break ranks, but to hold their positions.

From the back of his charger Duke William watched in horror as the left side of his front disintegrated and hundreds of screaming Saxons came running headlong toward the Norman lines. Now the left centre of his line began to slip backward and the centre wavered between advance and retreat, and the duke was instantly struck by the disastrous possibility of a total collapse of his infantry and the sure defeat that would follow. He spurred his horse and rode quickly out in front of his

Norman chevaliers, who were mounted and standing ready for the next phase of the assault.

Shouting orders to Odo and Robert, at the head of the Norman cavalry units, he commanded the chevaliers to move out and wheel to their left and rush into the path of the running, screaming Saxon soldiers who were pursuing the fleeing Bretons.

The Norman chevaliers immediately spurred their mounts and sped off to intercept the English fyrdmen who were dashing across the meadow at the west side of the battlefield. The cavalry's movement also served to block the impending retreat by other elements of the Norman front. Within moments the horsemen rode into the Englishmen, crashing their horses into them and trampling them and with lances and swords wielded from atop their mounts, spearing and slashing the hapless Englishmen, most of them armourless fyrdmen. Those who turned back toward their shield wall to escape the slaughter were soon overtaken by the chevaliers and hacked or speared to the ground. Entire units of fyrdmen from the right side of the English line were wiped out, their men left dead or dying where they fell on Senlac meadow.

The horsemen wheeled again and galloped back to the Norman lines while Duke William rode to the left side of his line to speak sharp words to the Breton soldiers who by now had safely regained their original position near the foot of Telham Hill.

Count Alan of Brittany pointed his sword toward the English line and ordered the Breton infantrymen back across the meadow, and they ran off to resume the attack.

The duke then raced back to the centre of his line and shouted new orders, launching the third phase of the Norman assault.

Even above the din, the trumpets from the Norman side of the field could be heard along the English line. When they sounded, the invaders' infantrymen disengaged from the fight at the shield wall and started moving back.

Moments later trumpets sounded again from across the meadow, and with the first notes of the call, the entire host of Duke William's horsemen, thousands of men and mounts, in ranks that stretched from the bog in front of the patched-up English right to the marsh in front of the English left, set off at a gallop, then spurred their animals into a run, gathering speed, charging rapidly across the meadow, thousands of hoofs sounding like rolling thunder as the huge and awesome horde, with lances poised, pounded directly toward the English line, racing between and among the withdrawing infantrymen.

It was a sight unseen before by the men of the shield wall, who fought man to man, on foot, in the faces of their enemy, eye to eye. The sight and sound of the charging horses, terrifying in their numbers, in their enormity and speed, bearing armoured warriors, set off a wave of dismay along the line of defenders.

The horses pounded right up to the English line, their riders hurling lances into the defenders' ranks then drawing swords to slash the defenders, or couching their lances in an underhand grip and thrusting into the shield wall.

Axe-wielding housecarls immediately struck back. They quickly realised the horses, unprotected by armour, were the first enemy to be dealt with and they turned their axes on them first, slicing their legs from beneath them, cleaving their big heads from their shoulders, opening giant gashes in their bellies, dropping them like timber all along the English front. Unhorsed riders fought to save themselves and to press the axe-wielding Saxons back. Many succeeded in saving themselves, many failed. All failed in pressing the axe wielders back. According to one account, the first Norman rider to be killed was a favourite of Duke William, the minstrel Taillefer, whose rich singing voice had taunted the English as he reached their line. He paid for his daring with his life, as did hundreds of other chevaliers.

After some twenty minutes of furious butchery, the invaders' cavalry broke off the assault and withdrew across the meadow. Horseless chevaliers, many of them bloodied, walked or hobbled back among their mounted comrades, as riderless and panicked horses raced wildly through the mounted and dismounted mass of horses and men.

On the English side of the meadow, for a distance of about thirty yards in front of the shield wall and along its entire width, the ground was strewn with the bodies of the invaders' dead and wounded, and so many horse carcasses lay along the English line that they became an irregular barricade, a new aid to further defence of the shield wall.

Immediately in front of the shield wall and within its first ranks lay King Harold's fallen defenders, many hundreds of them. And now, at about 11.30 a.m., during the lull in the battle, as the combatants rested and those who felt like eating fed themselves on their rations, both sides began collecting their dead and carrying their wounded behind their lines to do as much as could be done for them. On the English side, the care of the wounded was a task given mostly to the women, many of them the wives, daughters and mothers of the men fighting. The Normans had brought monks, some of whom were physicians as well, to care for their wounded and pray over the dead.

The dead gave up their armour. On both sides, unarmoured fighters stripped hauberks from armoured corpses and tugged them onto themselves, knowing the battle was far from over. Lances and spears and other weapons were retrieved from the ground where they had landed, to be used again.

About 12.30 p.m. Duke William ordered a new assault. Again his companies of archers marched from the regrouped formation and at about one hundred yards began shooting into the English line, with the same small effect on the shield wall. Again with their quivers emptied, they retired to their own lines.

Now Duke William himself rode out in front of the mass formation, while the archers were still making their way back across the meadow, and he shouted to Odo and Robert, who in turn shouted orders, and on the sounds of trumpets, the foot soldiers marched out again toward the English line and the first rank of cavalry moved out seconds later, the infantrymen separating to allow the horses through their ranks.

Near the centre of the line of chevaliers rode William, his standard bearers riding with him, charging toward the shield wall, the turf beneath them already churned with the hoofs of so many horses galloping across the meadow and back. As the horsemen drove their mounts into the wall of shields, thrusting with lances, the duke slowed his mount and took a command position just behind the leading chevaliers, turning his charger to the right to ride to the spot where the horsemen of the Franco-Flemish division were beginning to assault the English line; the running, shouting foot soldiers now reaching the shield wall and throwing themselves against it with sword and spear.

Axe-wielding housecarls again hewed and hacked down the invaders' horses, then turned their weapons on the unhorsed riders while thanes and fyrdmen launched lances and spears at the invading infantrymen, then drew swords and stood with shields before them to repel the attackers as they tried to penetrate the wall.

Suddenly, amid the fierce hail of projectiles and the storm of blows from axe and sword, Duke William went down as he rode behind his front ranks, he and his horse disappearing from the view of all but those close by him. As soon as he went down, his standard bearers immediately reined in their horses, quickly dismounted and sprang to where he and his black charger lay sprawled on the ground.

Shouts then went up from the infantrymen who had seen him go down and had watched his standard bearers, Turstin and Tosteny, dismount and drop beside the duke.

'*Le duc est mort!*'

As the shouts were repeated, the right centre of the attackers' line began disengaging from the shield wall, horsemen and infantry alike, and turning in confusion toward the sound of the shouts. Count Eustace, on horseback at the left rear of the Franco-Flemish division's troops, heard the shouts, too, and seeing the first signs of alarm and disengagement, spurred his mount and rushed toward the spot where the duke's standards were still flapping above the heads of the fighters.

By the time he got there, in a matter of moments, Duke William was on his feet and ordering his standard bearers to find him another horse. Beside him the black charger lay dead from a lance in its flank and a *coup de grâce* struck by the duke with his mace.

The count raced to the rear to wave for a new mount for the duke, then turned back to the wavering line of attackers and started shouting, telling the duke's troops that he was not dead and urging them to fight on.

Within a few minutes William was astride a fresh horse, his standard bearers beside him, and was joining in the shouts. He lifted his helmet so his men could recognise him.

Heartened, the duke's troops pressed harder against the English line even while Saxon axes were repelling their advance with a fierce defence that refused to be breached and, though weakened by the continuous assault, was wreaking horrible losses on the invaders.

After nearly two hours of slaughter and mayhem, Duke William ordered his army to disengage and withdraw back across the meadow. The English line, bloody and diminished but still standing together, unbroken, cheered as the defenders watched the enemy fall back.

Harold, at the rear of the English ranks, likely had no doubt that the Bastard would come again. He would keep coming till he had nothing more to come with. Harold was determined that he would make William spend every last man trying to break the English line, and when he finally failed, Harold's army would send the Bastard to hell, or back to Normandy if he was fast enough to escape.

At about 3.30 p.m., Duke William launched his third assault. Once more his archers stepped out from the regrouped formation and moved within range of the English line, closer this time than before. Then the foot soldiers and cavalrymen again moved out together, their numbers reduced by the two previous assaults, but still an awesome force as they moved resolutely toward the shortened and thinned Saxon shield wall.

The horsemen and foot soldiers streamed past the archers as they stood in position about eighty yards from the English line. Then as chevaliers and infantrymen neared the shield wall, the archers lifted their bows skyward, to effect a high trajectory, and let their arrows fly, shooting over the heads of their comrades dashing toward the English line, raining arrows down on the defenders.

Again the invaders struck the English line with lances thrust by mounted chevaliers and swords wielded by armoured infantrymen. Again the men of the shield wall fought them off, arm-weary fighters on both sides struggling to make one last effort before a setting sun would grant them merciful relief from a day of slaughter.

On Duke William's right flank the French and Flemish fighters of Count Eustace's division were meeting particularly stubborn resistance from the English holding that end of the ridge, the swords and axes of the defenders mangling the ranks of attackers as they pressed up the slope, till at last the invaders on the extreme right flank of the duke's front turned and in confusion began running back down the slope.

Berserk yells went up from the left end of the English line, which suddenly snapped forward like a whip end, rushing out from the shield wall to pursue the fleeing French and Flemish, believing victory was now within their grasp.

Duke William, observing from atop his horse at the centre rear of his lines, instantly reacted. He ordered his Norman cavalry and the remnants of the Franco-Flemish cavalry to turn quickly and drive on the surging left flank of the defenders, who were running wildly after the retreating invaders, thereby collapsing the left end of the shield wall.

As they had earlier done to the fyrdmen on the opposite end of the broad English front, the Norman chevaliers swiftly cut down the defenders spilling down the slope, then, seeing the advantage they had with the left side of the shield wall collapsed, spurred their mounts up the slope, into the tattered left flank of the English, past the defenders' line and up onto the top of the ridge.

Gyrth was perhaps the first commander to see the turning of the English flank. With his shield in front of him and brandishing his sword, he yelled to his housecarls to shift to their left to stem the rush of the Norman cavalry, now riding across the top of the ridge, headed toward the centre of the English formation, rolling up the left side of the shield wall. With Leofwine not far behind him, Gyrth ran to meet the onrushing chevaliers.

William's mounted knights turned aside Gyrth's housecarls, taken by surprise, and galloped past and over the defenders, who were now faced with an enemy behind them and in front of them. Rushing past the resistance, the chevaliers met Gyrth on foot and struck him to the ground, then drove lances through him.

Yards behind Gyrth, with a handful of his own housecarls hastily pulled from the shield wall, Leofwine, also on foot, attempted to blunt the chevaliers' thrust. His meagre force was quickly overcome by the mounted Normans, and Leofwine was killed by chevalier swords as he stood in the path to Harold's command post, fighting to block the Normans' advance toward the king.

Around King Harold a contingent of housecarls stood guarding him. With little warning or time to prepare, the king's bodyguard was suddenly confronted by the onrushing Norman chevaliers, riding speedily toward the command post from the left. One of the body-guard jumped in front of Harold to shield him. Just as he did, a new wave of Norman arrows came hurtling down on their position, and one of them struck Harold's protector in the right eye, its steel point piercing his brain, and he fell dead at Harold's feet.

Immediately the Norman horsemen swarmed onto the small band of the king's bodyguard, who fought fiercely with axe and sword to defend the command post. King Harold grabbed up the battleaxe of one of the wounded housecarls of the bodyguard and swung it into the leg of a chevalier and the right flank of his mount. As he did, he was caught on the shoulder by a chevalier's sword and dropped to the ground. When Harold fought to regain his feet, the chevalier struck him again, repeatedly, dismounting when he saw that Harold had gone still. Then, standing over the dead king, he continued to slash and chop at Harold's body, dismembering it.

After that, the Norman cavalry, pouring in from the left side of the shield wall, rode up and down the rear of the English line, shredding it, till the front had been burst and breached repeatedly and all defenders had fallen or fled, their wounded hacked to pieces where they fell, the survivors and those who had cared for the wounded running for their lives down the north slope of the ridge, dashing pell-mell for the safety of the woods beyond Caldbec Hill or for the protection of a gully, later to be called the Malfosse (Evil Ditch), that lay to the north of their former position on the ridge.

The Normans' pursuit of the Englishmen was halted by one furious but futile last stand by the defenders at the Malfosse and by darkness, now falling fast on the bloody slopes of Senlac Ridge.

22

THE AFTERMATH

15 OCTOBER–25 DECEMBER 1066

T he duke was outraged. In the late afternoon's fading light, at the site of the English command post atop Senlac Hill, he was staring at a corpse so mutilated that he couldn't say for sure that it was Harold's. The duke demanded the name of the person who had committed this atrocity.

Someone suggested it would be a good idea to get a positive identification of the body, to make sure it was indeed Harold and not someone mistaken for Harold. William accepted the suggestion and ordered a search for someone who knew Harold really well. Perhaps there was some old mark on his body or some other identifying feature, something that someone very close to him could find and say for certain this was Harold. William would look again at the scattered remains, the disembowelled body, the severed head and slashed face, the severed leg and severed genitals. Then he would walk away, shaking his head.

It didn't take long to learn who the men were who had ravaged King Harold's command post. Twenty chevaliers had been in the first group to turn the English left flank and race across the rear of the English line. Four of them had survived the fierce English attempt to stop them and to protect the king. Those four were Ivo of Ponthieu, the son of Count Guy of Ponthieu; Walter Giffard the younger; Hugh of Montfort; and Count Eustace himself. All four had participated in the deaths of Harold and his bodyguard. All apparently had been questioned about the killing of Harold. Ivo had admitted the mutilation.

William ordered him brought to him, and Ivo came, likely expecting to be rewarded. The duke, who had granted Ivo knighthood, unleashed his anger on him now. He denounced his actions and him personally. He stripped him of his knighthood and ordered him out of the Norman camp immediately, banishing him in disgrace back to Ponthieu.

At this point legend fills in the place left empty by the historical record. It says that Duke William did find someone who had known Harold well and could identify the body. She perhaps had come to the Norman camp, in the company of canons from Waltham Abbey, to ask for the body so that it could be given a Christian burial.

Edith Swan's Neck was able to identify the mutilated remains as Harold's, perhaps an old, odd scar on his torso providing the conclusive evidence. Harold's remains were removed from Senlac meadow and taken by the canons to the abbey at Waltham, one of the places Harold loved best in all of England, where they were buried in a spot no longer marked or known.

From his field of triumph outside Hastings, Duke William moved on to complete his conquest of a leaderless England. He marched his army, diminished by the loss of an estimated 2,500 men and 600 horses, to Canterbury, which promptly surrendered to him, then to Winchester, which also surrendered, then finally, at the completion of a long, circuitous route, to London, encountering only weak and scattered resistance as he went and ravaging the towns and countryside where he met opposition.

He intimidated London into capitulation and thus captured the nation's political and economic capital, the symbol of its nationhood. After that, most of the nation's remaining leaders, including its archbishops, submitted to him, and on Christmas Day 1066, in Westminster Abbey, William, whom history would come to call the Conqueror, was crowned king of England.

True to the promises he had made to those he had recruited to help him gain the English crown, he systematically dispossessed England's landowners and turned over their properties, their farms, estates and cities to the men who had helped him win his decisive victory at Senlac Ridge.

Cruelly suppressing all challenges to his rule, William remained king until his death in Normandy on 9 September 1087. He was succeeded by his son. More than nine centuries later, another of his descendants, one in a long line of successors, reigns as England's monarch today.

Finis

CHRONOLOGY

1000 BC (or earlier)
Celts invade and occupy the British Isles, supplanting late Stone Age inhabitants.

55 BC
Julius Caesar leads a Roman expeditionary force into Britain.

AD 43
Romans invade and begin their subjugation and occupation of Britain.

*c.*400
Angles, Saxons and Jutes begin migrations into Britain.

410
Romans withdraw from Britain.

700–1000
Vikings raid British coasts, overrun and settle in areas of England, Scotland and Ireland.

911
Viking chief Rolf (Rollo) is ceded Normandy by the French king and becomes the first
duke of Normandy.

1002
King Aethelred of England marries Emma, daughter of Duke Richard of Normandy.

1004
Edward, son of Aethelred and Emma, is born.

1013

Prince Canute of Denmark unsuccessfully attempts to depose Aethelred. Queen Emma takes refuge in Normandy with sons Edward and Alfred.

1016

Aethelred dies. Canute proclaims himself king of England. He makes Godwin an earl.

1017

Emma returns to England, leaving sons Edward and Alfred in Normandy, and marries King Canute.

1028

William is born.

1035

Canute dies. Harold Harefoot, Canute's son by his first wife, declares himself king of England. Duke Robert of Normandy, father of William, dies.

1036

Prince Alfred, Edward's younger brother, dies after having his eyes gouged out by Godwin's men.

1040

Harold Harefoot dies. Harthacanute, Canute's son by Emma, becomes king of England. At the invitation of Harthacanute, his half-brother Edward returns to England from Normandy.

1042

Harthacanute dies. Edward becomes king of England.

1045

Edward marries Edith, daughter of Godwin.

1051

Godwin and his family are banished by King Edward.

1052

Godwin, aided by his sons Harold and Tostig, assembles an army and navy, and forces Edward to capitulate and restore to him and his sons and daughter their former titles and property. Duke William marries Matilda, daughter of the count of Flanders.

1053

Godwin dies.

1055

Edward appoints Godwin's son, Tostig, earl of Northumbria.

1057

Earl Leofric of Mercia dies. His son Aelfgar succeeds him as earl.

1063

Armies led by Harold and Tostig defeat King Griffith of Wales on behalf of King Edward.

1064

As King Edward's envoy, Harold travels to Normandy to meet with Duke William.

1065

Northumbrians rebel against Tostig. Edward confirms rebels' choice of Morkere, son of Aelfgar, to be the new earl of Northumbria. Tostig and his family sail to Flanders for refuge.

January 1066

Edward dies. Harold is crowned king of England.

Spring 1066

Leading an army of mercenaries, Tostig conducts hit-and-run raids on England's southern and eastern coasts.

June 1066

Tostig makes an alliance with King Harald Hardrada of Norway to attempt an overthrow of Harold.

July 1066

Duke William moves to quarters at the mouth of the River Dives to oversee the assembly of his invasion fleet and army.

7 September 1066

Combined forces of Harald Hardrada and Tostig launch an invasion of England.

20 September 1066

Harald Hardrada and Tostig defeat armies of Earls Morkere and Edwin at Battle of Gate Fulford.

25 September 1066

Harold and his army defeat Harald Hardrada and Tostig at Battle of Stamford Bridge.

28 September 1066

William and his invasion force land at Pevensey, England.

14 October 1066

Harold and his army are defeated by William and his invaders at Battle of Hastings.

25 December 1066

William is crowned king of England.

ABOUT THE BOOK'S SOURCES

I n the 1960s, when the so-called 'new journalism' writers (Tom
Wolfe, Gay Talese, Rex Reed, Barbara Goldsmith, George
Plimpton, Hunter S. Thompson and others) began using storytelling devices (*fiction* devices, some said) in what they wrote for maga-
zines and newspapers, thereby endowing their pieces with a gripping
power expected at that time to be found only in novels, some traditionalists in the word business cried 'foul'. Their horrified feeling was,
as Tom Wolfe characterised it, 'The bastards are making it up!'

Of course they were doing no such thing. The anecdotes, the scenes,
the descriptive detail, the dialogue, the characterisation had all come
from their reporting. It was factual. They were simply using all that
material to make their stuff more readable. That was the main idea of
using storytelling technique – to make what they wrote interesting
enough to be read. And who could legitimately fault them? After all,
what was – what still *is* – the point of writing, if not to be read?

Faced with history texts that read like stories (instead of like history
textbooks), some book editors today register the same sort of reaction
as those traditionalists who read in horror the new journalism in the
1960s: 'He's making it up.'

He's not. He's just trying to make history as readable as possible,
because he wants it to be read as widely as possible. History doesn't

have to be dull. It never did. The best, the most memorable history book I read as a young student is one that I still remember, William H. Prescott's *History of the Conquest of Mexico*, written as dramatic narrative and first published in 1843.

Since history occurs chronologically, why not, when possible, write it chronologically, like a story? Since history is stories of things that have happened to people and things done by people, why not tell it as stories? Telling stories, after all, is the world's most effective form of communication, and communication is the writer's ultimate goal.

Doubts persist, though. Maybe some are justified, particularly when a text offers neither footnotes nor endnotes, the primary purpose of which is not to be read by the general reader, who is likely to find them a distraction, but to provide verifying documentation (and to reassure editors that it's not made up).

In researching *Harold & William*, I drew material from more than forty sources and I now happily, eagerly acknowledge my debt to all of them, especially those from which I drew the most. With all possible sincerity I hereby express my deep, deep gratitude to those authors, editors and translators whose works made such large contributions to this story of Harold and William. Their names and their works are acknowledged under the Selected Bibliography on page 187 of this book.

For the information of this book's readers, moreover, it's probably important that they know something about the story's original sources, to give them some knowledge of where the material first came from. Those sources are the ones to which all modern writers on the subject of the Norman Conquest have directly or indirectly resorted and on which they have depended for the substance of their works. Surely foremost among those original sources is the fabulous Bayeux Tapestry, which presents, in fascinating, colourful, historic detail, the story – or at least *a* story – of Harold and William. Flawed by occasional ambiguity, some obvious inaccuracies and an intentional bias throughout, the tapestry is nevertheless the prime source of material concerning the rivalry between Harold and William. It provides the backbone of the story – the story line itself – and uncounted precious visual details as well. The tapestry, which dates back to about 1080, is very much like an eleventh-century equivalent of a modern documentary on the events associated with William's conquest of England. It is a treasury of historic material. (For an exciting aesthetic and educational experience, Internet users can view the entire tapestry, section by section, in vivid colour and detail at www.hastings1066.com.)

Two biographies of William, authored by Normans, are among the chief written sources for the story of Harold and William. They are *The Deeds of William, Duke of the Normans and King of the English* (*Gesta Guillelmi ducis Normannorum et regis Anglorum*), written by William of Poitiers about ten years after the Battle of Hastings, and *The Deeds of the Duke of the Normans* (*Gesta Normannorum Ducum*), written by William of Jumièges about five years after the battle.

Other original sources are: *Ecclesiastical History* (*Historia Ecclesiastica*), written by an Anglo-Norman monk, Ordericus Vitalis, around 1140; *Song of the Battle of Hastings* (*Carmen de Hastingae Proelio*), written by Guy, bishop of Amiens, in the year after the battle; and *The Anglo-Saxon Chronicles*, written by anonymous monks, the entries relevant to the story of Harold and William having been written probably not many months following the Battle of Hastings.

The major source for the parts of the story of Harold and William having to do with King Harald Hardrada of Norway and Harold's brother Tostig is the highly readable and richly detailed *Heimskringla*, the saga of King Harald written, apparently from the oral tradition, by Snorri Sturluson around 1230. (The translation I have is the one by Magnus Magnusson and Hermann Palsson, titled *King Harald's Saga*, an enjoyable and rewarding piece of reading.)

Other old sources from which modern writers have taken material include: *The Life of King Edward* (*Vita Aedwardi Regis*), an anonymous work written approximately in the years 1065–1067; *Domesday Book*, an anonymous work that dates to around 1086; *A History of the Kings of England* (*De Gestis Regum Anglorum*), written by William of Malmesbury around 1124; *History of the English* (*Historia Anglorum*), written by Henry of Huntington about 1130; *Roman de Rou*, written by Robert Wace about 1160; and *Life of Harold* (*Vita Haroldi*), an anonymous work written around 1216.

From a practical point of view, however, credit as sources should go mostly to the modern writers, editors and translators whose efforts have created documents that are more easily accessible, more concise and more helpful than are those old works, and which in most cases include indexes. Those works are the sources this author depended on most heavily and to whom his debt of gratitude is greatest. They especially include: *William the Conqueror*, by David C. Douglas; *Edward the Confessor*, by Frank Barlow; *1066, The Year of the Conquest*, by David Howarth; *The Enigma of Hastings*, by Edwin Tetlow; *The Making of the King, 1066*, by Alan Lloyd; *Hastings*, by Peter Poyntz Wright; *1066, The Story of a Year*, by Denis Butler; and *Invasion: 1066*, by Rupert Furneaux. Readers who would like to read more on the subject of the Norman Conquest will find any or all of these works both illuminating and satisfying.

And now, a final word. Borrowing a pleasant custom from the prodigious historian Will Durant, who ended most of the eleven volumes of his monumental *The Story of Civilization* with a brief note of thanks to his readers, I would very much like to thank each reader of this book for having come this far. For your interest and your patience, I am truly grateful.

B.R.P.

SELECTED BIBLIOGRAPHY

The author is immensely indebted to, and hereby expresses his deep gratitude to, those whose work made this book possible. They include:

Barclay, C.N., *Battle 1066* (Van Nostrand: Princeton, 1966)

Barlow, F., *Edward the Confessor* (University of California: Berkeley, 1970)

Bender, B., with Caillaud, R., *The Archaeology of Brittany, Normandy and the Channel Islands* (Faber & Faber: London, 1986)

Cathcart Borer, M., *The City of London* (David McKay: New York, 1978)

Brent, P., *The Viking Saga* (Putnam: New York, 1975)

Brooke, C., *The Saxon and Norman Kings* (Collins/Fontana: London, 1967)

Butler, D., *1066 The Story of a Year* (Putnam: New York, 1966)

Calder, N., *The English Channel* (Viking: New York, 1986)

Dottin, G., *The World of the Celts* (Minerva: Geneva, 1977)

Douglas, D.C., *William the Conqueror* (University of California: Berkeley, 1964)

Erickson, A.B., & Havran, M.J., (eds), *Readings in English History* (Scribner's: New York, 1967)

Fisher, D.J.V., *The Anglo-Saxon Age* (Barnes & Noble: New York, 1992)

Franklyn, J., *Heraldry* (A.S. Barnes, Cranbury: New Jersey, 1965)

Furneaux, R., *Invasion: 1066* (Prentice Hall: New York, 1966)

Garrett, R., *Clash of Arms, The World's Great Land Battles* (Galahad: New York, 1976)

Gibbs-Smith, C.H., *The Bayeux Tapestry* (Phaidon: London, 1973)

Haigh, C., (ed.), *The Cambridge Historical Encyclopaedia of Great Britain and Ireland* (Cambridge University: Cambridge, 1985)

Bannister Harding, S., & Fletcher Harding, W., *The Story of England* (Scott, Foresman: Chicago, 1909)

Held, R., (ed.), *Arms and Armor Manual* (Follett: Chicago, 1974)

Howarth, D., *1066, The Year of the Conquest* (Penguin: New York, 1981)

Humble, R., *The Fall of Saxon England* (St Martin's: New York, 1975)

Lloyd, A., *The Making of the King, 1066* (Dorset: New York, 1966)

Madsen, O., *The Vikings* (Minerva: Geneva, 1976)

Magnusson, M., & Palsson, H., (trans.), *King Harald's Saga*, from Snorri Sturluson's *Heimskringla* (Penguin: New York, 1966)

Muntz, H., *The Golden Warrior* (Scribner's: New York, 1949)

Norman, A.V.B., *The Medieval Soldier* (Crowell: New York, 1971)

Norman, A.V.B., & Pottinger, D., *English Weapons & Warfare, 449–1660* (Barnes & Noble: New York, 1992)

Palmer, A., *Kings and Queens of England* (Octopus: London, 1976)

Poyntz Wright, P., *Hastings* (Windrush: Gloucestershire, 1996)

Savage, A., (trans.), *The Anglo-Saxon Chronicles* (St Martin's/Marek: New York, 1983)

Simon, E., *The Anglo-Saxon Manner* (Cassell: London, 1972)

Smurthwaite, D., *The Complete Guide to the Battlefields of Britain* (Barnes & Noble: New York, 1993)

Stenton, D.M., *English Society in the Middle Ages* (Penguin: Harmondsworth, 1951)

Strickland, M., *Anglo-Norman Warfare* (Boydell: Woodbridge, Suffolk, 1992)

Tetlow, E., *The Enigma of Hastings* (St Martin's: New York, 1974)

Warner, P., *The Soldier, His Daily Life Through the Ages* (Taplinger: New York, 1976)

Whitelock, D., *The Beginnings of English Society* (Penguin: Harmondsworth, 1952)

Whitelock, D., Douglas, D.C., Lemmon, C.H., & Barlow, F., *The Norman Conquest, Its Setting and Impact* (Eyre & Spottiswoode: London, 1966)

Williamson, J.A., *The English Channel, A History* (Collins: London, 1959)

Also the authors of *The Westminster Abbey Official Guide* (Peebles: New York)

INDEX

Adela, Countess (daughter of
  Robert I of France) 69
Aelfgar (son of Earl Leofric) 40, 41
Aelfgarsdottir, Lady Alditha 41, 50,
  84, 85, 86, 112, 128
Aelfgarson, Earl Edwin, of Mercia
  40, 41, 42, 43, 45, 48, 49, 50, 51,
  53, 58, 81, 84, 85, 86, 100, 102,
  112, 121, 122, 123, 128, 133, 158
Aelfgarson, Morkere, earl of
  Northumbria 40, 41, 42, 43, 44,
  45, 48, 49, 50, 51, 53, 58, 81, 84,
  85, 86, 100, 102, 112, 121, 122,
  123, 128, 133, 134, 158
Aelfwig (King Harold's uncle) 158
Aethelred the Unready 34
  Viking raids on England 33
  marriage to Emma 20
Alan of Brittany, Count 165, 170
Alexander II, Pope 54, 75, 92, 161
Alfonso of Aragon (King) 161
Alfred, Prince 31, 34
Anderida (Roman fortress) 146, 149
Andreadsweald, forest of 158
Ansgar (sheriff of Middlesex) 158
Avranches, town of 26

Baldwin V, count of Flanders 45, 69,
  96, 106
Beachy Head 146, 147, 148
Beaurain, castle of 20
Bexhill, town of 147, 150
Birsay, Brough of 117
Bonneville-sur-Touques, castle of
  70, 72, 73
Bosham Manor 15, 16, 37, 38, 47,
  48, 50, 111, 112
Brede, River 147, 158, 159
Bresle, River 20, 21
Brighton, town of 99

Brionne, siege of 72
Bulverhythe, port of 147, 150

Caesar, Gaius Julius 64, 65, 66, 67,
  68, 77, 83
Caldbec Hill 158, 159, 160, 162, 176
Canmore, Malcolm III (King of
  Scotland) 36, 101, 102, 117, 118
Canute (King) 31, 40, 45, 87, 97,
  106, 154
  claim to the English throne 34
Cassivellaunus (Celtic chieftain) 65
Charles the Simple (King of
  France) 23
Chichester, port of 15
Conan, count of Brittany 25, 27,
  28, 95, 96
Cospig (Tostig's deputy) 40, 100,
  101, 137
Couesnon, River 25, 26

Danelaw 38
Dapifer, Gerald 79
Deauville, port of 73
Derwent, River 128, 129, 130, 132
Dinan, siege of 28
Dives, River 13, 109, 147
  estuary of 109, 110, 139, 140, 141
Dol, siege of 25, 26, 27, 28
Dolfinson, Ulf, thane of
  Northumbria 37, 39, 97
Dover, port of 32, 57, 79, 83, 99, 147
Dover, Strait of 63, 64
Duncan I (King of Scotland) 101
Dunfermline, town of 102, 118

Eadwig, Prince 34
Waltheof, Earl 58, 157, 158
East Anglia 48, 100, 154
Edith Swan's Neck 15, 17, 24, 35,

36, 37, 38, 39, 40, 45, 47, 48, 50,
  51, 52, 111, 112, 178
Edward, Prince 31, 34
Edward, the Confessor (King) 9, 11,
  15, 19, 20, 21, 24, 31, 32, 34, 36,
  37, 39, 42, 43, 44, 45, 54, 57, 73,
  83, 92, 98, 147, 154
  death of 53, 54
  illness of 34, 41, 47, 49, 50, 51, 52
  relationship with Harold 17, 47,
    48, 49, 51, 60
  relationship with Queen Edith
    47, 52
  relationship with Tostig 35, 40, 41
  speech to Harold on deathbed
    51-2
Eldred, archbishop of York 54, 55,
  56, 85
Elizabeth (wife of Harald and
  daughter of King Jaroslav) 104,
  105, 106, 113, 114, 116
Emma (Queen) 20, 33, 34, 73
English Channel 10, 11, 13, 16, 17,
  20, 25, 56, 59, 62, 63, 64, 66, 67,
  68, 73, 77, 86, 97, 101, 109, 110,
  125, 126, 127, 130, 134, 139, 146,
  147, 152
Enguerrand de Ponthieu 18
Estrith (sister of King Canute) 97
Eu, town of 20, 21
Eustace, Count 165, 173, 174, 177

Faber, William 165
Firth of Forth 102, 117, 118
Forest of Dean 49
Fridrek (King Harald's standard
  bearer) 135

Gate Fulford, battle of 123, 127,
  128, 156

Giffard, Walter 24, 79, 177
Gilbert of Lisieux 89
Gloucester, city of 49
Godwinson, Edmund 37
Godwin (father) 31, 32
Godwin (son) 37, 50, 51, 98, 158
Godwinson, Gyrth 13, 31, 35, 44, 48, 50, 58, 81, 126, 127, 153, 154, 157, 162, 163, 175
Godwinson, Gytha 37
Godwinson, Harold (King) 7, 8, 9, 10, 11, 12, 13, 14, 15, 16, 17
  accompanying William to Dol 25, 26, 27
  acknowledgement of Earl Morkere on behalf of king 45
  affection for Waltham 154
  asking Edwin and Morkere for support 48, 49, 50, 86
  burial at Waltham 178
  coronation of 54-5, 56
  cure at Waltham 154
  death of 175
  description of army/navy 81, 83, 157, 164, 167
  establishing headquarters at Isle of Wight 110
  excommunication 152
  formation of army at Hastings 162, 163, 164
  formation of army at Tadcaster 127
  gathering his brothers at Bosham Manor 48
  Harold's possible capture by Guy de Ponthieu 18, 19, 20, 21
  identification of dead body 177, 178
  interceding with Tostig on Edward I's behalf 35, 36, 38, 39, 42, 43
  journey to solicit successor from Normandy 16, 17, 18, 21, 23, 24
  marches to Caldbec Hill 156-7, 160, 162
  marriage to Alditha 85
  masses army at London 127, 157
  meeting with the witan 87-8
  mercy on Norwegian prince 138
  mutilation of body 176, 177
  Norman knighthood 29, 30, 31
  oath to William 31-2
  offers of peace to Tostig 132, 133, 136
  omen at Waltham 155
  parleying with Northumbrian rebels 42, 43
  preparation for battle of Stamford Bridge 129, 130
  preparations for William's invasion 83, 84, 97, 125
  rallying troops at Hastings 164
  reaction to alliance between Tostig and Harald 112
  reaction to battle of Gate Fulford 126
  reaction to Edward I's illness and death 48-54

  reaction to Gyrth's advice 153, 162
  reaction to Harald and Tostig's invasion 126, 127
  reaction to Northumbrian rebellion against Tostig as earl 35-43
  reaction to William's invasion 151, 152, 163
  reactions to Tostig's raids 99, 111
  reconnaissance at Hastings 160
  refusal of William's terms of peace 153-3
  refusal to let Gyrth lead the army 153, 162, 163
  refusal to wait to amass whole army 151, 154
  relationship to Alditha 50, 85, 86, 87, 112
  relationship with Edith Swan's Neck 24-5, 36, 38, 48, 50, 51, 111, 178
  relationship with Edward I 16, 17, 34, 35, 36
  relationship with his brothers 13, 31, 35, 42, 44, 47, 126, 162
  response to Malet 80, 81
  response to William's envoy 152, 153
  securing York with army 128
  summoning the fyrd 111, 125, 126, 157
  support for Harold 52-4, 58, 86, 127, 178
  support of Archbishop Stigand 52, 53, 54, 74
  thoughts on succession 47, 48
  victory at Stamford Bridge 136-7, 138, 151
  visit to York 84, 85
  warning Edith of danger 111
  witan proclaim king 53
Godwinson, Judith (wife of Tostig) 39, 45, 96
Godwinson, Ketel (Tostig's son) 129, 137
Godwinson, Magnus 37
Godwinson, Skule (Tostig's son) 129, 137
Godwinson, Tostig, earl of Northumbria 11
  attacking York 119
  claiming of hostages at York 123-4
  death of 136
  defeat by Aelfgarsson brothers 100, 101
  defeat of English at Gate Fulford 120-123
  desertion by army 101
  first invasion of England 98
  flight to Flanders 44
  mismanagement of earldom of Northumbria 35, 36, 37, 40, 41, 42, 44
  overcoming Northumbrian fyrd 122, 123
  raids on coastal towns 98, 99

  relationship with Harold 13, 42
  relationship with Judith 39, 44
  relationship with Queen Edith 36, 39, 44
  rendezvous with Harald 117
  second invasion of England 117-8
  seeking alliance with King Sweyn 96
  seeking alliance with Malcolm III 101
  seeking alliance with William 96, 97
  temperament 35, 38, 44
Gospatric, thane of Northumbria 39, 40
Griffith ap Llewellyn (King of Wales) 35, 41, 50, 85
Guy de Ponthieu 9, 10, 18, 19, 31, 177
Guy of Burgundy 72

Hadrian, Emperor 118
Hailsham, town of 149
Halley's Comet 88
Hardrada, Magnus 106
Harefoot, Harold (King) 34
Harthacanute (King) 34, 106
Hastings, battle of 8, 10, 83
Hastings, town of 99, 147, 148, 149, 150, 152, 153, 158, 159, 160, 161, 163, 178
Henry I (King of France) 18
Herluin (monk) 72
Hildebrand (archdeacon of Rome) 90, 91, 92, 93
Hrossey, port of 116
Hugh of Avranches 24, 71, 79
Hugh of Grandmesnil 24
Hugh of Montfort 79, 177
Humphrey of Tilleul 149

Ironside, Edmund 34
Isle of Wight 16, 97, 98, 110, 111, 112, 125
Ivo of Ponthieu 177, 178

Jaroslav (King of Novgorod) 104
John of Ravenna 24

Lady Godiva (wife of Earl Leofric) 40
Land Ravager (Landeyda) (emblem) 119, 122, 135, 136
Lanfranc (abbot) 72, 73, 74, 75, 89, 90, 91, 92
LeBec-Hellouin, abbey of 72
Leofric, Earl of Mercia 40, 50
Leofwine, Earl (brother of King Harold) 35, 44, 48, 50, 58, 81, 126, 127, 153, 157, 175
Leopards of Normandy (Norman flag) 166
Lillebonne, castle of 77
Loire, River 96

Macbeth (King of Scotland) 101
Magnus (King), son of Olaf 105, 106, 114

Malet, William, lord of Graville-
Sainte-Honorine 60, 80
Malfosse (Evil Ditch) 176
Margot, Hugh 152, 153
Matilda (William the Conqueror's
wife) 21, 69, 70, 71, 72, 96, 97,
140
Mercia, earldom of 40, 42, 51, 53,
84, 86, 100, 102, 112, 123, 127
Mont St Michel, Bay of 26
Mora 71, 140, 141, 143, 145, 146, 148

Nicholas (abbot of St Ouen) 79
Nicholas II, Pope 70, 72
Nidaros (Norwegian capital) 113
Normandy 10, 11, 17, 18, 19, 20, 23,
24, 25, 32, 34, 37, 53, 56, 59, 62,
77, 79, 80, 88, 95, 96, 109, 110,
141, 147, 165, 174, 178
Norse raven (battle emblem) 66
Northumbria, earldom of 35, 36, 38,
40, 41, 42, 43, 44, 45, 51, 53, 84,
86, 87, 96, 100, 102, 112, 118,
119, 123, 124, 126, 127, 132, 134,
152

Odo, bishop of Bayeux 10, 23, 29,
58, 79, 143, 165, 169, 172
Olaf, Saint (King of Norway) 103,
104
Orkney Islands 100, 101, 113, 114,
116, 117, 118, 138
Ormson, Gamal, thane of
Northumbria 37
Orre, Eystein 116, 121, 122, 123,
129, 131, 136, 137
Oswulf, Earl 58
Ouse, River 38, 120, 121, 122, 129,
138

Petley Wood 162
Pevensey, town of 99, 146, 147, 148,
149, 151, 152, 153
Philip of France (King) 79

Quevilly, estate of 57

Ralph of Toesni 24
Rance, River 28
Rasyphus, Saint 30, 161
Ravennus, Saint 30, 161
Remigius, Bishop 79
Rennes, castle of 96
Riccall, town of 120, 122, 123, 124,
127, 128, 129, 130, 131, 136, 137,
138
Richard I, Duke 26, 33, 95
Richard II, Duke 20, 33
Richard of Evreux 24, 79
Riwallon, lord of Dol 25, 27, 28
Robert of Jumieges (archbishop) 74
Robert the Devil 19, 23, 34
Robert, count of Eu 20, 21, 58, 79
Robert, count of Mortain 58, 79
Roger of Beaumont 24, 71, 79
Roger of Montgomery 24, 71, 79
Rolf/Rollo (Viking chieftain) 23,
69

Rolloson, Turstin 166, 173
Rouen, town of 12, 23, 26, 28, 29,
57, 72, 93, 96, 109, 140

Santlache Hill 163
Scapa Flow 117
Scarborough, town of 119, 120, 121,
126
Seine, Bay of 16, 17, 109, 141
Seine, River 16, 17, 23, 57, 77
Selsey Bill 16
Selsey Cathedral 16
Senlac Hill 8, 13, 14, 163, 165, 170,
176, 177, 178
Shanklin, town of 98
Shoreham, town of 99
Sigurdsson, Harald Hardrada (King
of Norway) 11, 13, 36, 47
accession as King of Norway 105
alliance with King Sweyn 105
appoints Magnus co-king 114
attacking York 123
betrayal of King Sweyn 97, 105
death of 135
defeat of English at Gate Fulford
123
description of 103, 104, 106
fleet sets sail 115-6
invasion of England 118-9
invasion of Sicily 104
marriage to Elizabeth 105
marriage to Thora 106
overcoming Northumbrian fyrd
123
peace with King Sweyn 105
pilgrimage to Jerusalem 104
preparations for invasion 114
relationship with Elizabeth 104,
113
rendezvous with Tostig 116
support for Tostig 106, 107, 112
use of daughters to win support
of Orkney earls 113
visit to Malcolm III 118
visit to Olaf's shrine 114-5
wins support of Torfinnson earls
116, 117
Sigurdsson, Ingegerd (daughter of
King Harald by Elizabeth) 106,
113
Sigurdsson, Magnus (son of King
Harald by Thora) 106, 114
Sigurdsson, Maria (daughter of
King Harald by Elizabeth) 106,
113, 138
Sigurdsson, Olaf (son of King
Harald by Thora) 106, 114, 122,
123, 129, 137, 138
Siward, Earl 35
Sogne fjord 114, 115, 116
Somme, Bay of the 141, 142, 143
St Clement, church of 115
St Peter the Apostle, church of 52,
54
St Stephen's Abbey 72
St Valery, port of 141, 142, 147
St Valery-sur-Somme Abbey 142
Stamford Bridge, battle of 13, 130,

132, 134, 137, 138, 151, 157, 159
Stamford Bridge, village of 128, 129
Stigand, archbishop of Canterbury,
52, 53, 54, 55, 74, 75, 87
Stiklestad, battle of 104
Sturluson, Snorri 11, 132, 133, 185
Styrkar (King Harald's chief of staff)
116
Sweyn of Denmark (King) 97, 105,
106

Tadcaster, town of 120, 127
Taillefer (minstrel) 171
Telham Hill 160, 162, 163, 164, 165,
168, 169, 170
Thora (King Harald's second wife)
106, 114, 116
Thorbergson, Nicholas 116, 121,
123, 137
Thorney Island 49
Thurkill (commander in King
Harold's army) 158
Tofig the Proud 154, 158
Torfinnson, Erlend (earl) 113, 116,
117, 118, 121, 129, 137, 138
Torfinnson, Ingebjörg (mother of
Paul and Erlend/wife of
Malcolm III) 117
Torfinnson, Paul (earl) 113, 116, 117,
118, 121, 129, 137, 138
Trondheim, palace of 113, 114, 115
Tynemouth, village of 118

Ushant, islet of 63

Val-es-Dunes, battle of 19
Varangian Guard 104

Waltham Abbey 10, 154, 155, 178
Wessex, dragon of (battle emblem)
16, 26, 134, 164
Wessex, earldom of 15, 35, 58, 81,
86, 98, 99, 126, 157
Westminster Abbey 49, 52, 53
Westminster Palace 34, 39, 45, 53,
80, 87, 99, 178
Westminster, city of 37, 47, 49, 84,
126, 155
William fitz Osbern, lord of
Breteuil 23, 24, 29, 58, 78, 79,
143, 165
William of Poitiers 9, 10, 24, 185
William of Warenne 24
William, the Conqueror, duke of
Normandy 8, 9, 10, 11, 12, 13,
14, 17, 18, 19, 20
allegations against Harold 74
alleged murder of Conan 96
assembling army 109
believed dead at Hastings 173
celebration of Mass 159
conference in Normandy 77
coronation of 178
death of 179
decision to invade England 58
description of army/invasion
fleet 139, 140
dispatches Lanfranc to Pope 75

entertaining Harold 23, 24
falling over on beach 149
flaws in William's claim to
  English Crown 48, 73
fleet caught in storms 141
fleet sets sail from Bay of the
  Somme 143
fleet sets sail from Dives 141
granted papal support for
  invasion of England 92, 93, 152,
  153
headquarters at Dives 109
invitation of Harold to Dol 25,
  26
knighting of Harold 28, 29
landing at Pevensey 146, 147, 148
march to battle at Hastings 160,
  161
march to London 178
marriage to Matilda 21, 69
Mora parted from rest of fleet
  146
motivation for pursuit of English
  Crown 22
oath to Harold 30, 32

offer of Agatha in marriage to
  Harold 24
prayer to St Valery 142
praying on battlefield at Hastings
  164, 165
preparations for invasion 66, 68,
  71, 77, 79, 80, 110, 140, 145
punishment of Ivo 178
ravaging English countryside 150,
  154
reaction to Harold's coronation
  57
reaction to Harold's death and
  mutilation 177
rebuffs Tostig's alliance 96, 97
reconnaissance at Pevensey 146,
  147, 149
relationship with Matilda 69, 70,
  71, 72, 140
rescue/reception of Harold 20,
  21
response to Harold's arrival 23,
  24
resting at St Valery 141, 142
rewarding followers 178

sending envoy to Harold in
  London 150, 152, 153
sending Gilbert of Lisieux to
  Pope Nicholas 89, 90
sending Harold's spy back to
  England 110
sending Malet to England 60
summoning closest allies 58
summons Lanfranc 72
victory at Hastings 175, 177
winning support 78, 79
Witan 17, 32, 38, 40, 42, 49, 50, 51,
  53, 56, 73, 84, 85, 87, 88, 124
Witanagemot 43, 53
Wulfstan (bishop of Worcester) 85,
  87

York Cathedral 85
York, city of 38, 40, 84, 85, 87, 119,
  120, 121, 122, 123, 124, 127, 128,
  129, 130, 137, 138, 151, 154, 157

Zoe, empress of Byzantium 104

If you are interested in purchasing
other books published by Tempus, or in case you have
difficulty finding any Tempus books in your local bookshop,
you can also place orders directly through our website

www.tempus-publishing.com

or from

BOOKPOST
Freepost, PO Box 29,
Douglas, Isle of Man
IM99 1BQ
Tel 01624 836000
email bookshop@enterprise.net